EGYPTIAN·BOOKSHELF

PAPYRUS

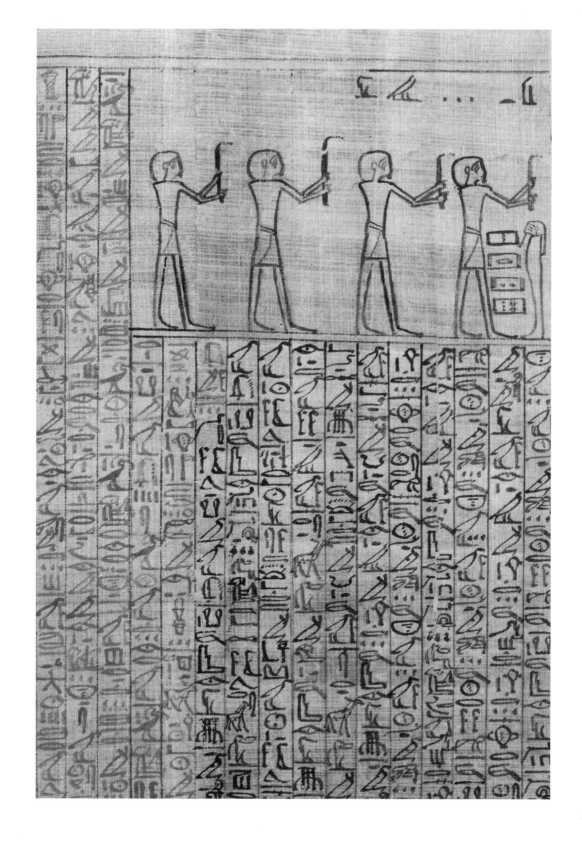

EGYPTIAN · *B*OOKSHELF

PAPYRUS

RICHARD PARKINSON &
STEPHEN QUIRKE

With contributions by
UTE WARTENBERG & BRIDGET LEACH

Published for the Trustees of the British Museum
by British Museum Press

© 1995 The Trustees of the British Museum

Published by British Museum Press
A division of British Museum Publications Ltd
46 Bloomsbury Street
London WC1B 3QQ

British Library Cataloguing in Publication Data is available

ISBN 0-7141-0979-7

Designed by Grahame Dudley Associates
Typeset by Create Publishing
Printed in Great Britain by the Bath Press, Avon

Front cover: Example of a fine hieratic hand from the longest surviving Egyptian papyrus. Twentieth Dynasty, c.1150 BC; from Thebes. Detail from Papyrus Harris, EA 9999.78.

(Frontispiece) Detail from the papyrus containing the Book of the Dead of Nu. The cursive hieroglyphic text is illustrated by a vignette in which four schematically rendered men bear torches toward a mummified figure and four 'magic bricks' to be placed around the burial chamber. Early Eighteenth Dynasty, c.1400 BC. H. of torch-bearers 5.9 cm. BM EA 10477.26, detail.

Contents

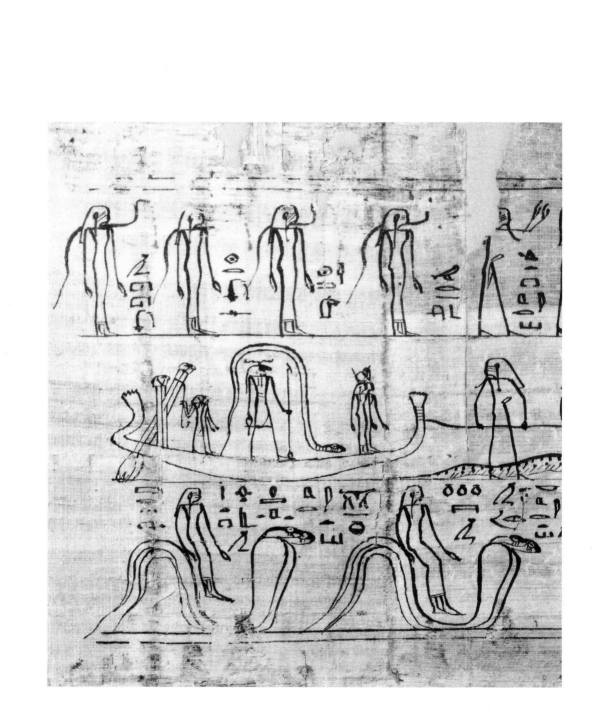

Acknowledgements

In surveying such a vast range of material as is preserved on Egyptian papyri, omissions are inevitable. We have tended to concentrate on the periods and areas of Egyptian documentation in which we are most experienced, while trying not to lose a broader perspective. The preparation of the text has been divided between us not by sections but by stages. Ute Wartenberg has contributed immeasurably to the book's discussion of classical papyri and papyrology (especially the first half of chapter 4), and Bridget Leach likewise to the discussions of manufacture and conservation. We are greatly indebted to them for much invaluable instruction, helping our partial knowledge. Carol Andrews has provided us with a great deal of aid concerning demotic. We have drawn heavily on papers by Alan Donnithorne and John Tait; we are also very grateful to Eve Menei for much advice. John Baines and John Tait have very kindly read drafts and offered extensive comments and corrections. The remaining errors are, of course, our responsibility.

Part of an Underworld Book, *the* Amduat, *in which the bark of the sun-god is drawn by deities through the night. The figures are drawn in schematic outline. Third Intermediate Period, c.950 BC, from Thebes. H. of roll 23 cm. BM EA 9975, detail.*

Thanks are owed to our editor Sarah Derry. Much of the photography has been undertaken by Janet Peckham; we are grateful to Dr Harrauer of the Austrian National Library for supplying the photograph of the Persian papyrus, and to the Royal National Theatre for the photograph from *The Trackers of Oxyrhynchus*. The maps and some of the figures are by Christine Barratt.

Lastly, Richard Parkinson wishes to express his gratitude to T.G. Reid, *spirto leggiadro*, for moral support and much else.

R.B.P.

S.Q.

March 1994

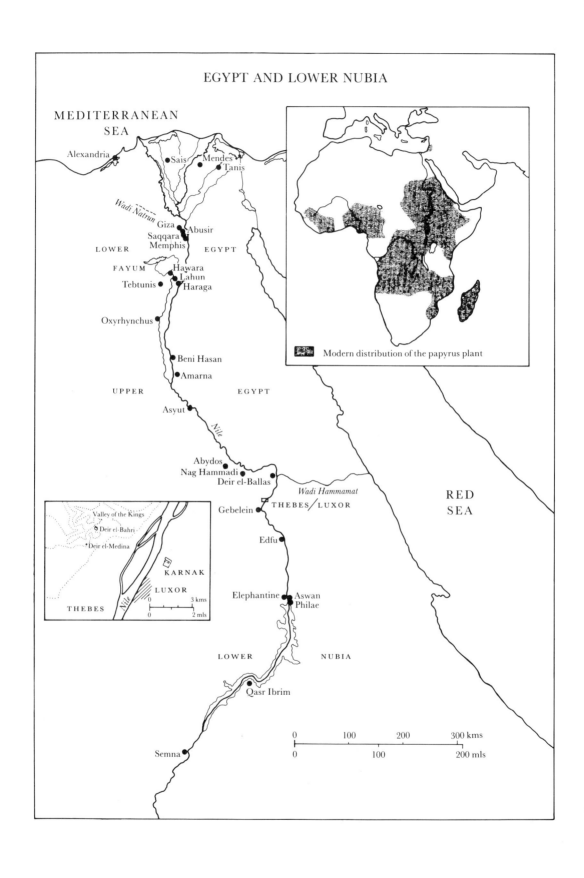

EGYPT AND LOWER NUBIA

MEDITERRANEAN
SEA

Alexandria

Sais

Mendes
Tanis

Wadi Natrun

Giza
Saqqara Abusir
Memphis

LOWER   EGYPT

FAYUM   Hawara
                    Lahun
Tebtunis   Haraga

Oxyrhynchus

Beni Hasan

Amarna

UPPER   EGYPT

Asyut

Nile

Abydos
Nag Hammadi
Deir el-Ballas

Wadi Hammamat

Gebelein   THEBES/LUXOR

Edfu

RED
SEA

Elephantine   Aswan
               Philae

LOWER   NUBIA

Qasr Ibrim

Semna

Modern distribution of the papyrus plant

Valley of the Kings
○ Deir el-Bahri
• Deir el-Medina

KARNAK

LUXOR

THEBES   0   3 kms
                0   2 mls

Nile

0   100   200   300 kms

0   100   200 mls

CHAPTER ONE

Natural History and Manufacture

Papyrus growth not in Englande, it hath the facion of a greate Docke…
It maye be called in englishe water paper; or herbe paper
Turner, Names of Herbes *(1548), 20.*

About AD 70, Pliny the Elder described the papyrus plant and its use as a writing surface in his *Natural History*. He introduced his account with the words:

The nature of papyrus too is to be recounted, for on its use as rolls human civilisation depends, at the most for its life, and certainly for its memory.

Pliny was thinking of the Roman world, but his remarks can be applied to the early Byzantine and Islamic empires, the classical Greeks and the Persians, Palestine and Syria in the later second and first millennia BC, and of course the ancient Egyptian state: some four thousand years from *c*.3100 BC onwards. Papyrus provides a vast source of evidence about its homeland of Egypt, ranging from literary masterpieces to laundry lists, and a rare opportunity to hear the voices of the long dead.

The writing material papyrus is made from a tall flowering freshwater reed, generally identified as *Cyperus papyrus*, which flourishes in tropical Africa along the water's edge. Its range of habitats runs from the tropical to the temperate. The exact sub-species within the sedge family is difficult to identify. The original reed itself had died out in the Egyptian Nile valley by the time of the French expedition of 1798–1801 under Napoleon Bonaparte (which produced the first modern description of the flora), although it seems to have grown continuously in the southern Sudan, where it still flourishes. A papyrus type was reintroduced to Egypt in 1872 from botanical gardens in Paris, but it is uncertain exactly where this originated, and these French specimens perhaps came from the colonialist exploration of central to eastern Africa, rather than from

1 *Map of Egypt, with an insert showing the modern distribution of the papyrus plant.*

Egypt. Within the Mediterranean area varieties of papyrus still grow wild in Sicily and the Jordan valley, but it is not known when the plant reached those regions.

The ancient writing material cannot be easily identified botanically from the surviving examples because it is made from the core of the plant stem, which may not vary greatly from one sub-species to another. Without the precise plant type, details such as the rate of reproduction remain unknown. The chemical composition of the papyrus plant varies between sub-species or between specimens grown in different places and this can affect its suitability for a specific use. Analyses have revealed differences between examples grown in Egypt and in European botanical gardens. Another factor which can change plant type is cultivation, which might have played a part in the plant's history at periods of concentrated use. Despite these difficulties, the general characteristics of the papyrus family give us an overall picture of the plant and its potential for making a writing surface similar to modern paper.

Although papyrus had disappeared from the Egyptian Nile valley, a strain was found growing wild in 1968 in the Wadi Natrun, an oasis area immediately west of the Delta. This strain shows some characteristics of Sicilian papyrus and some of Sudanese papyrus, and might be a late survivor of the ancient Egyptian plant. In experiments it has not produced a writing surface as successfully as that from the strain introduced from Paris in the nineteenth century. This, however, may only reflect the advantages of the cultivated over the wild plant.

Cyperus papyrus consumes great quantities of water and therefore grows most successfully in the still shallows of marshlands. Its broad root stretches horizontally under the mud and from this rise several strong stalks, triangular in section; short brown leaves protect the base. Papyrus is by far the tallest of the botanical genus *Cyperus*, growing to a height of as much as five metres, its nearest rival being no more than two metres high. In the Roman Period the writer Strabo described the ancient Egyptian plant as about three metres tall. At its tip the stalk splits into a mass of strands (the 'umbel'), and at the end of these the plant produces small brown flowers, except in the depths of winter.

The triangular stalk of the papyrus plant has a tough green rind which conceals a white pith composed of a mass of cells with occasional vascular bundles, the vegetable equivalent of arteries, which carry water and sustenance from the root to the flowering head.

WORDS, IMAGES AND USES

In the ancient Egyptian language the plant was called either *mehyt*, which was perhaps a general word for marsh plants, or the more specific *tjufy*. The latter survived into the Egyptian of the Christian period as *djoouf*. The ancient Greeks used two words, *papuros* and *bublos*. In the fourth century BC the writer Theophrastus used *papuros* when referring to the plant used as a foodstuff and *bublos* for the same plant when it was used to make artificial products, whether rope, basketry or a writing surface. Ptolemaic Greek texts kept this distinction but the word *papuros* tended later to denote any marsh reed; some Classical texts mention *papuros* in Greece and mainland Italy, but these probably refer to marsh reeds in general, as there is no solid evidence that papyrus grew in either area. The Greeks usually called papyrus rolls *chartes*; the Romans transferred the Greek terms into their own script as papyrus and *charta*. In Arabic the most common word for papyrus is *bardy*.

The origin of the word 'papyrus' itself is not known, but it may derive from a late Egyptian phrase *pa-en-peraa*, 'material of Pharaoh', perhaps because trade in the writing material was under royal control in the third century BC. However, no Egyptian text ever uses the phrase. Modern European words for paper derive from the Greek *papuros*; the Italian 'carta' is from the Latin *charta*, and can refer to paper, although other languages have taken from it other meanings such as 'card' and 'cartography'. The Greek term *bublos* is supposedly derived from the place name Byblos, a major Phoenician port for ancient Mediterranean trade through which the material might have reached Greece. In modern European languages it has spawned a series of words connected with books, from the 'Bible' to 'bibliophile'.

In Egypt the most extensive marshes were in the north and the plant became the emblem of Lower Egypt used in iconographic motifs such as the scene of 'Uniting of the Two Lands', in which two heraldic plants were bound together. The plant was regarded as so typically Egyptian that in broader contexts it could be a metaphor for the whole country in contrast to foreign lands. In the *Tale of Sinuhe* from the Middle Kingdom the hero is in voluntary exile in Syria-Palestine and in his despair he remarks, 'what can fasten the papyrus to the mountain?', meaning that Egyptian culture is incompatible with the surrounding desert highlands. In the hieroglyphic script a stylised papyrus stem wrote words for 'green' and 'flourishing' (in Egyptian *wadj*), and the sign was used as an amulet that was important enough to merit its own spell in the *Book of the Dead*. *Wadj*-amulets were worn by the living as well as the dead, as recent excavations by the British Museum at the town sites of Ashmunein and Balamun have shown. In iconography, the same shape occurs as a sceptre held by goddesses.

Because of its height and dense growth in thickets, the plant is a haven for wildlife, especially birds. The wildlife and the luxuriant greenery of the papyrus marshes made them the Egyptian equivalent of the European pastoral landscape in art and literature. They also had a religious dimension, symbolising the emergence of the land from the primordial swamp, a site of primeval power. Fishing and fowling expeditions were not just for necessity or pleasure, but were also courtly and religious acts, celebrating victory over the potential chaos of nature. The hunting scene is an enduring motif in Egyptian art: in the tombs of courtiers a depiction of a hunting trip served to secure rebirth by evoking this triumph. In tomb

II

chapels of the Old Kingdom scenes show papyrus stalks being shaken in a ritual. Here, the tomb owner has made a journey into the marsh thicket and is sometimes represented uprooting and shaking a single papyrus stalk as if to frighten birds into the air before hunting. Sometimes, two stalks were plucked and shaken in honour of Hathor, the goddess of sexuality. The sound was considered similar to that of the sistrum, a rattle-like metal musical instrument used in cult and particularly associated with Hathor. Plucked papyrus stems were also used in bouquets for rituals and banquets.

2 The plant was very important in everyday life; it was put to numerous practical uses from sandal-making and basketry to the construction of river craft, as the Greek writer Herodotus noted in the fifth century BC. He mentioned the making of sails and papyrus rope (which was widely used in the Mediterranean and features in Homer's *Odyssey*) and he recorded that the lower part could be eaten, particularly when roasted. This was presumably the water-logged root, and although there is no ancient Egyptian written evidence for this, roots have been found in excavation. Surviving examples of rope, sandals and basketry show the uses of the tougher parts of the plant. Tomb scenes show men gathering stems, mostly for making boats. A similar scene occurs on a papyrus from the Late Period alongside other pastoral activities (BM EA 9961).

Although the majority of the population would have used the plant only for these purposes, its most inventive use was as a writing surface – perhaps the most influential achievement of the ancient Egyptians. The *Hymn to the Inundation*, probably composed in the Middle Kingdom,

2 *Sandals and chest made out of papyrus fibre. New Kingdom, c.1300 BC; from Thebes. Chest H. 23 cm, EA 5918, sandals L. 23.5 cm, EA 26781.*

acknowledges the importance of papyrus in its list of the benefits of the inundation:

all writings of hieroglyphs
(are) the Inundation's work, being from the reeds.

HARVEST AND PRODUCTION

Egyptian scenes show papyrus stalks being pulled out of the root, bundled together and tied, and carried off for use. There is no record from Pharaonic times of the seasons of cultivation or harvest. Two contracts for private leases of papyrus plantations from the first century BC indicate that wild marshes yielded material for matting and the like, while special plantations met the massive demand for writing material across the Roman Empire. In one contract, the lessees pay double rent for the period March to August, implying that production peaked in the summer months. From September the annual flooding of the Nile raised the water level to its maximum height, submerging the swamps more deeply and complicating access to the crop. In modern revivals of papyrus-making, it is generally cut in the spring, although better results have been obtained from slightly older papyrus cut in the early summer.

Not only is there little information on crop production, but there are no ancient Egyptian representations or texts on the production of papyrus sheets and rolls, and no papyrus workshop has ever been identified in excavations. Manufacture was described at length by Pliny the Elder in his *Natural History*, but the description is now difficult to follow, and has given rise to various interpretations.

First, a stem of papyrus was cut into manageable lengths. After, the rind was peeled off and a stem then cut or peeled apart. It is uncertain whether the core was cut into several strips or was peeled into a single thin layer. Peeling has been proposed recently by I. H. M. Hendriks as the most likely method, a suggestion also advanced by Samuel Birch in 1878. A sheet made from strips would have a lattice-like effect, as is seen in modern pieces of papyrus rather more so than in ancient examples. Peeling would have avoided this effect, though it might have produced an unevenness in quality from one side of the peeled layer to the other, because the part nearer the rind contains more vascular bundles than the

3 *Scene from the tomb-chapel of Puyemra, showing a man peeling rind from a harvested papyrus stem. Early Eighteenth Dynasty, c.1400 BC; painted plaster, Thebes. After a drawing by N. Garis Davies.*

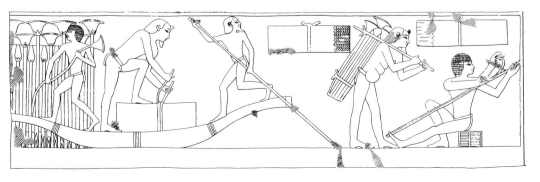

part at the core. These vascular bundles appear in each strip or peeling as thicker fibres running the length of the stem, and are a characteristic of all papyrus sheets. It is likely that, in practice, combinations of cutting and peeling were used, depending on various circumstances. The differing appearance of papyri of different dates suggest that the precise techniques also varied from one period to another.

4   Once peeled into sheets or cut into strips, the material was laid in two layers at right angles to each other and forced together to form a single rectangular sheet, making sure that no gaps appeared between the strips. Produced in this way, a sheet had one side with the stem fibres running from top to bottom (vertical fibres) and one with them running run from right to left (horizontal fibres). When a sheet was rolled, it tended to preserve its shape better if the vertical fibres were on the outside. For this reason the Egyptians used the side with horizontal fibres uppermost as the front of the sheet, where they would start writing, while the side with vertical fibres uppermost inevitably took the brunt of any dirt or damage to the roll. The front of a sheet (horizontal fibres uppermost) is now usually known as the 'recto' while the back (vertical fibres uppermost) is the 'verso'. In general, a sheet was slightly thicker than modern writing paper. Two layers of fibres were sufficient, although a possible example of a three layer Greek papyrus has been noted. This is a fragment of a de luxe copy of the *Iliad* and the extra layer is apparently not due to a

4 (Top row) Three suggestions of how papyrus pith was cut: the first, cutting from one side (Ragab method); the second, cutting from three sides (a method suggested by Corrado Basile); the third, unpeeling (Hendricks method). The drawings (below) show how a sheet was produced by laying one row of strips at right angles across another.

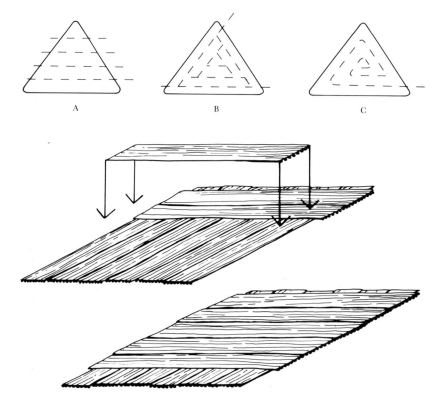

A   B   C

sheet-join or a repair. A Pharaonic example is the *Book of the Dead* of the priestess Nestanebetisheru (Twenty-first Dynasty, BM EA 10554), which was claimed to be three-layered when it was first published (it was then mounted on paper and the claim is now difficult to check). Another three-layer fragment was reported from a *Book of the Dead* in the University Library in Leipzig.

It seems that no glue was needed to join the layers. The strips of papyrus were not allowed to dry out before they were joined, and this seems to lie behind Pliny's statement that immersion of the sheet in Nile water gave the adhesion. In modern Sicilian papyrus an additive is introduced to help adhesion but other papyrus makers have relied on the adhesive properties of the natural composition of the plant. Hassan Ragab, a modern Egyptian papyrus manufacturer, has argued that the bonding of the fibres is due not to saccharides in the cell sap but to a physical bonding of the cell tissue of both layers.

Another unresolved question concerns the application of pressure to join the strips. Pliny referred to presses; these are used in modern manufacture but it is also possible that in Egypt the layers were simply hammered together. The preparation of a roll certainly involved vigorous action: in a Nineteenth Dynasty model letter a scribe tells his apprentice to work hard at his profession, rather than share the lot of the soldier, who is 'laid out, beaten like a papyrus roll, and violently thrashed'. It is unclear whether the beating is to fuse strips into a sheet or to join sheets into a roll.

The edges of the sheets varied in neatness but were usually foursquare, not rhomboid. After manufacture, the sheets were glued together with a flour paste to form a roll. The joins were generally right over left on the recto, which suited the usual direction of writing since the pen would not be obstructed by the extra overlapping layer(s) of the next sheet. If the writing was in the other direction the roll would be held up the other way. In the demotic papyri of the fourth century BC from North Saqqara, as John Tait notes, a fringe of horizontal strips had been left projecting beyond the vertical strips when the sheets were manufactured. This

5, 26, 33, VI

5 A papyrus roll of five sheets, with a strengthening strip at the start (right). The sheet-joins are visible as lines running the height of the document; they are right over left (with an overlap of about 1 cm) following the direction of the text, a demotic contract. Ptolemaic Period, 230 BC, from Thebes. H. 31 cm. EA 10074.

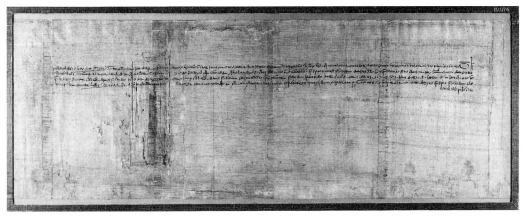

6 An unopened papyrus roll. The visible end demonstrates how compactly a papyrus could be rolled. It is stained by resin, suggesting that it was placed beside a mummified body. Thirtieth Dynasty or Ptolemaic Period, c.300 BC (?), from Thebes. H. 29.2 cm. EA 10748.

would have allowed a smoother sheet join (with three layers rather than four in the overlapping join); in some early papyri the joins are very difficult to detect. From a list of donations inscribed on the walls of the temple of Ramses III at Medinet Habu, it seems that the standard roll was twenty sheets long. According to Pliny, this was the maximum length for rolls in the Roman Period, and rolls of this length are also found in the early Islamic Period. The contents of a single Middle Kingdom roll would be roughly equivalent to 7 pages of this book.

SIZE AND FORMAT

The breadth of sheets varied in size from 38 to 42 cm in the Middle Kingdom, and 16 to 20 cm in the New Kingdom. It was the height of the sheet that determined the content of a roll. Manuscripts of full sheet height would have been costly and also cumbersome for a Pharaonic scribe to handle when he was writing on his lap; thus papyri taller than 30 cm were used only in special contexts such as the royal chancellery or the studios where funerary papyri were produced. Rolls of full height were usually halved or even quartered lengthwise to produce more convenient sizes. From the Old Kingdom, surviving accounts measure between 21 and 24 cm high, and these are presumably half of an original full height roll measuring 42 to 48 cm. Other accounts of the same period are 11 to 15 cm high, a quartered roll. Middle Kingdom accounts documents and some literary manuscripts present a format of 30 to 33 cm in height, which seems to have been the full-height roll for that period. Around the beginning of the New Kingdom this format was used for a group of technical texts (the medical Papyrus Ebers, now in the University Library, Leipzig, and the Rhind Mathematical Papyrus (BM EA 10057/8), 30 cm and 32 cm high respectively). Most surviving literary manuscripts of the Middle Kingdom are half-height rolls at 16 cm, or quartered rolls at 8 cm.

Eighteenth Dynasty papyri from the reign of Thutmes III are slightly larger, with accounts texts 36 cm high, halved to 16 to 17 cm for literary texts. In the Nineteenth to Twentieth Dynasties still taller rolls were produced, and some full-height examples of these survive (in contrast to the Old Kingdom). Most full-size accounts papyri measure 40 to 42 cm in height, but one, (BM EA 10403), reaches 45 cm, and another, the official record of works at Deir el-Medina, is 47 cm. Half-height rolls from both 40 cm and 48 cm originals survive, generally with accounts texts. Quarter-height rolls at 10 cm include the literary *Tale of Truth and Falsehood* (BM EA 10682), and examples at 11–12 cm include accounts (for example BM EA 10447) and literary texts. The tallest papyrus known is 53.5 cm high and dates from the New Kingdom; it is now in University College London. Its use for construction drawings of a shrine explains its exceptional size.

In the demotic papyri from North Saqqara, a standard sheet size tends to be found for all types of text and the sheet lengths varied between 14 and 16 cm only. Demotic legal documents of the Ptolemaic Period were very spaciously written, suggesting that the scribe had used a roll of the standard size despite the brevity of his text.

The original colour of freshly prepared papyrus was usually depicted as ivory white in Egyptian paintings of scribes at work, and in painted hieroglyphs of the book-roll sign: . Classical authors refer to whiteness as a valued quality of fine sheets. The material darkens to a yellow-brown colour with age, a fact that was familiar to the Egyptians: the walls of the tombs of Amenhotep II and Thutmes III in the Valley of the Kings were painted to represent texts on papyrus, on a background of yellow. It is difficult to be sure how white it was originally but the whiteness was probably obtained by bleaching in the sun. Pliny stated that drying in sunlight was part of the manufacturing process and ancient papyrus can still be rebleached by sunlight. The writing surface is quite rough; although it is not very absorbent, it takes ink well without any preparation. If burnished, it becomes too smooth and the ink spreads. When fresh, a sheet of papyrus is not fragile or brittle and it is in fact very durable. There are examples of rolls used over several generations; one roll that was written in the early Nineteenth Dynasty was still strong enough over fifty years later for the scribe Qenherkhopshef to copy an epic poem, the *Battle of Qadesh*, on its verso (BM EA 10683). Several late antique authors refer to consulting papyri over three centuries old and more recently, one curator of the papyrus collection in the Egyptian Museum, Berlin, would demonstrate the flexibility of papyrus by unrolling and rerolling a three thousand-year-old roll.

The oldest surviving papyrus is a blank roll found in a box in the tomb of Hemaka, an official of King Den of the First Dynasty. At this early date, the manufacturing process was already perfected and there is no evidence of any experimental stage, although there had presumably been one. The methods of papyrus production remained essentially the same for four thousand years until paper, which originated in China, replaced papyrus in the Arab world after the eighth century AD. The quality of papyrus varied according to factors such as how thin the sheet could be made and how regular and close the fibres were in relation to one another. The closest analogy is with woven materials, such as linen and matting, for which the Egyptians used the words *meh*, 'coarse', and

7 (Left) Part of a papyrus roll containing tabulated accounts written in hieratic in red and black, from the archive of the pyramid-temple of king Neferirkara. The fine, translucent quality of the roll is typical of Old Kingdom papyrus manufacture. Late Old Kingdom, c.2300 BC, from Abusir. W. from the left edge to the vertical line 3.6 cm. EA 10735.3.

(Below) A papyrus sheet bearing a letter from a scribe named Meh. The criss-cross pattern of the papyrus fibres, vertical over horizontal, is clearly visible on this sheet. Nineteenth Dynasty, c.1250 BC, probably from Saqqara. H. 25.1 cm. EA 73666.

shema', 'fine'. Perhaps the finest papyri ever made were literary manu-scripts of the Middle Kingdom; in these the sheets are wonderfully thin and translucent, and the fibres form a dense, even, criss-cross network. Such high-quality sheets were reserved for prestigious texts such as works of literature or court documents. Government accounts of the same period were often written on papyrus of good quality, while letters and less important accounts or notes might be on coarser material (although some were on pieces torn from larger high-standard sheets or rolls). While every period displays such variation in quality, in general it seems that the earlier manuscripts were the finer. Papyri of the Roman Period often comprise sheets of thick, poorly arranged fibres, and the latest papyri of the Islamic Period, in Arabic, Greek and Coptic, are among the most ineptly made.

46, 47, 48

AVAILABILITY AND PRICE

Although the papyrus plant was abundant in the marshes, the techniques of manufacturing the writing material were almost certainly specialised. This, combined with the restriction of literacy to the elite, may have sufficed to concentrate production of papyrus sheets and rolls in a few workshops at specific sites. Since papyrus must be fresh when the layers are pressed together to form sheets, manufacture presumably took place close to the marshes where it grew. Pharaonic times yield no evidence for the location of any papyrus manufacture centres; most of the relevant Greek texts refer to the Delta, preeminently the area near Alexandria, but also Sais and Tanis, and farther south in the Fayum.

Almost nothing is known about the way in which a Pharaonic scribe obtained his writing materials. He may have been allotted papyrus by the state or have bought it from the state or from a papyrus manufacture workshop. Even when evidence is more plentiful, in the Ptolemaic and Roman Periods, the extent of involvement by the state is uncertain; at that date manufacture seems to have been a private enterprise under state regulation, presumably for quality control as well as security of supply. At all periods the reuse of papyrus was widespread and scholars such as Riccardo Caminos have assumed that papyrus cannot have been cheap. However, another, Jac Janssen, has noted that a roll had a price of 2 deben (equivalent to a large basket or a small goat) at the Ramesside village of Deir el-Medina and so could hardly be considered expensive. For most of classical antiquity, the cost of a roll was equivalent to a labourer's wages for one or two days, but in the higher levels of society where papyrus was most used this was probably little more than an incidental expenditure.

ALTERNATIVES

Papyrus was the main portable writing surface in Egypt, but there were alternatives. Writing boards, usually made of sycamore wood, were a part of the scribe's equipment. Until the end of the Eighteenth Dynasty these

8

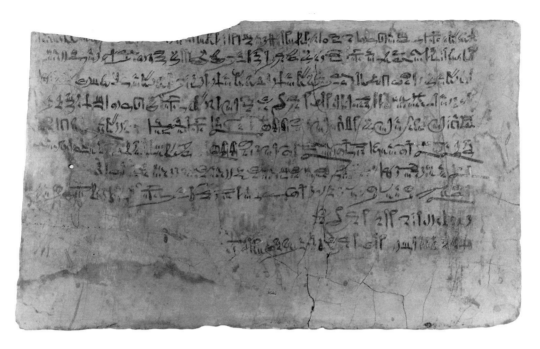

rectangular tablets were covered with a layer of white plaster and matched the maximum size of papyrus sheets. After the New Kingdom, plaster was no longer applied, and their size decreased. The tablets were pierced by a hole so that they could be suspended by a cord and hung from a peg for storage. They seem to have provided a more easily reusable surface than papyrus as they could be washed and replastered. Wax tablets familiar from the Roman world were not used in the Pharaonic Period, but tablets exist in other materials, and were presumably a substitute when wood was difficult to come by. There are, for example, limestone tablets principally from the late New Kingdom and the Ptolemaic and Roman Periods; these range in size from 31 x 18 to 9 x 6 cm. Unique examples of clay tablets from the late Old Kingdom have been found at Balat. These were incised with cursive script while still moist, reminiscent of later Cretan tablets. The reason for this substitution is clear: Balat is in Dakhla Oasis, which is remote from the centres of papyrus manufacture.

The most extensively preserved alternatives to papyri are 'ostraca': pot sherds or chippings of limestone. These were generally used for short texts which would have wasted papyrus. Some simple notes on flakes of limestone survive that show that the medium was already in use in the Old Kingdom. Stone and pottery ostraca are only slightly more commonly attested from the Middle Kingdom, surviving, for example, at the great fortresses in occupied Lower Nubia. In the Seventeenth Dynasty potsherds were used as ostraca and even whole beer-jars were used to write accounts. Complete vessels were used earlier to write 'Letters to the Dead'; here the purpose was to send a message to a recently deceased

8 *A wooden writing-board covered with plaster, bearing a hymn to Thoth. Note the hole at the centre of the left end. Early Eighteenth Dynasty, c.1450 BC, from Thebes. H. 26.7 cm. EA 5646.*

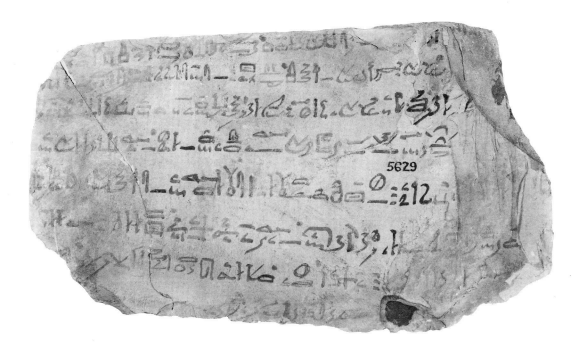

9 *Limestone flake or ostracon, bearing the final lines of the* Tale of Sinuhe *in black, with red 'verse points' marking verses, and a colophon in black. Nineteenth Dynasty, c.1250 BC, from Thebes. H. 17 cm. EA 5629.*

relative by writing the text on a vessel containing an offering for the spirit. However, an entire jar survives from the early Eighteenth Dynasty, (now in the Staatliche Sammlung Ägyptischer Kunst, Munich) which was used to write a letter to a living person. This resort to an unusual and somewhat inconvenient writing surface may reflect a shortage of papyrus. The use of other media is particularly well attested from the late Seventeenth Dynasty when the Delta-marshes were ruled by foreign kings from Western Asia; these surfaces might have been heavily used because the papyrus-producing centres in the north were inaccessible. Texts were also written on pottery vessels in the north at this time, as is shown by two jars with texts from a tomb at Haraga, at the mouth of the Fayum (now in University College London), but this usage may have been to do with the context, as the texts were funerary. The production of papyrus probably did not suffer a general decline at this period of disunity, since the few surviving papyri of this date show no loss of quality.

In the New Kingdom, ostraca continued to be used, and the vast majority are of limestone from a single site, the tomb-carvers' village of Deir el-Medina; the number is uncertain, but reaches well over 10,000. They contain transient notes and letters as well as numerous copies of literary texts. These may not have been permanent copies, however, as the excerpts are quite short; they may have been exercises in which apprentice scribes wrote out passages of prescribed texts. One extraordinary piece (now in the Ashmolean Museum, Oxford) is 31.5 x 88.5 cm and is a copy of most of the *Tale of Sinuhe*. Such a massive and thin piece of stone must have been carefully selected for the purpose, perhaps from the

cutting of a large tomb shaft. Most ostraca, however, were simply flakes of the rather poor local limestone.

Leather was an alternative to, rather than a substitute for, papyrus.
10 Leather is a more resilient surface in the short term but not over very long periods and the survival rate of leather manuscripts is poor. This makes it quite uncertain how much leather was used and in what contexts. Surviving leather rolls of the New Kingdom contain several different

10 *Part of the leather roll containing the* Book of the Dead *of the general Nakht. The text is in cursive hieroglyphs, reading from right to left unlike most funerary texts of this period. Above, a band of coloured illustrations show the judgement of the dead man, including the monstrous Eater of the Dead. Late Eighteenth Dynasty, c.1300 BC, from Thebes. H. 35.6 cm. EA 10473.2.*

types of text, from mathematical tables to illustrated *Books of the Dead*. The annals of Thutmes III, carved on the walls of the temple at Karnak, state that the full details of his campaign at Megiddo were 'recorded on a roll of leather (kept) in the temple of Amen'; this suggests that it was at least as prestigious a writing surface as papyrus. Although Pharaonic leather was treated, it was not as elaborately – or successfully – prepared as later parchment. Its preparation requires as much technical skill as papyrus.

Linen was also used as a writing surface, but only where linen was already being used and a text could be added as a secondary concern. One Old Kingdom 'Letter to the Dead' (now in the Egyptian Museum, Cairo) is on linen, and there are religious texts on votive offerings of cloth and funerary texts on shrouds in the Eighteenth Dynasty (e.g. BM EA 73807) and on mummy bandages (in the late Dynastic and Ptolemaic Periods).

CHAPTER TWO

Practical Usage

The scribes, gossips by nature and pedants by profession . . .
G. Maspero, Du genre épistolaire *(1872), 24*

SCRIPTS FOR PAPYRI

Egyptian hieroglyphs are elaborate pictorial signs which could be carved or painted in varying degrees of detail. They could be written from right to left or left to right, either vertically or horizontally. This flexibility suited their aesthetic role in monumental iconography but, from the beginning, there existed in parallel simplified forms written with a pen for daily records. The degree of cursiveness varied, depending on the status of what was being written. By the Middle Kingdom two separate styles of script had developed: a very simplified version of the pictorial signs, now known as 'cursive hieroglyphs', and a more abbreviated form termed 'hieratic', because it had come to be reserved for 'priestly' uses when the Greek historians visited Egypt.

Cursive hieroglyphs, although schematic, always retained something of the pictorial nature of the signs and were written separately. Occasionally, such as when they accompanied an elaborate opening illustration, they were drawn with almost as much detail as hieroglyphs on monuments (for example, the judgement scene in the New Kingdom *Book of the Dead* of Ani, BM EA 10470), and some were drawn with colour (for example, in the *Book of the Dead* of Qenna, now in the Rijksmuseum, Leiden). Cursive hieroglyphs were slower to write than hieratic and were thus more prestigious; they had slightly different rules of arrangement to hieratic and hieroglyphs. They were almost always written in vertical lines. In the hieroglyphic script, the signs mostly face towards the beginning of the text, but in most cursive manuscripts they face to the right, although the text was still read from left to right. This 'retrograde' writing may have emphasised the text's difference from other texts, and thus its sacredness. In one Middle Kingdom papyrus containing a kingship ritual

11

10, 12,
35, 36,
V, VI

11 *Egyptian scripts.*

Hieroglyphic Form	gem 'to find'	nub 'gold'	akhet 'flood season'
Cursive hieroglyphs			
Old Kingdom to early Middle Kingdom *c.3000–1900 BC* Hieratic			
Late Middle Kingdom *c.1900–1700 BC* Literary hieratic			
Administrative hieratic			
Second Intermediate Period *c.1700–1550 BC* Hieratic			
Early New Kingdom *c.1550–1300 BC* Hieratic			
Late New Kingdom *c.1330–1100 BC* Literary hieratic			
Administrative hieratic			
Third Intermediate Period *c.1100–700 BC* Formal hieratic			
'Abnormal hieratic' (Administrative hieratic)			
Late Period to Ptolemaic Period *c.700–30 BC* Late hieratic			
Demotic			

12 *An example of the cursive hieroglyphic script from a roll containing hymns to the crocodile-god Sobek (Papyrus Ramesseum 6). The text is in vertical lines (left to right); the title is written above in a horizontal band. Late Middle Kingdom c.1800 BC, from a tomb at Thebes. H. 13.5 cm. EA 10759.3.*

35   (BM EA 10610) there is a series of illustrations showing the participants with their speeches written above them; here the cursive hieroglyphs follow the rules governing captions in scenes from monumental art with the signs in the speech for each figure being aligned with him, whichever way he is facing.

The selection of a particular script for a papyrus was determined by the context, but a mixture of the two scripts might occur in a single archive of manuscripts. A collection survives from the tomb of a Thirteenth Dynasty priest (the 'Ramesseum papyri', see p. 62). In this, there were ritual
12   texts and hymns (to the god Sobek) written in cursive hieroglyphs. Of the rolls containing prescriptions and treatment texts, some were in cursive hieroglyphs and some in hieratic. The hieratic texts may have been personal copies. The cursive hieroglyphic documents were perhaps official copies originally from a temple library and acquired by the tombowner, possibly of the type termed 'festival roll' (ḥebyt) in texts. The 'bearer of the festival roll' was the lector-priest who recited rituals from a papyrus roll. Such rolls were perhaps generally written in cursive hieroglyphs in the Middle Kingdom. By the New Kingdom and Third Intermediate Period temple rolls could be written in hieratic, as extant copies
43   of the daily ritual for the god Amen show. In general, it can only be said that cursive hieroglyphic manuscripts were less accessible than hieratic, more sacred, and so more appropriate to a temple or royal library.
11   Hieratic was more abbreviated, angular and abstract than the cursive hieroglyphic script; for example, the body of a bird was reduced to a single line. Unlike cursive hieroglyphs, hieratic was almost invariably written from right to left. Most of the earlier hieratic texts were written in vertical lines, but horizontal lines became more usual during the late Middle Kingdom and vertical lines were rare after the early New King-

dom. By the second half of the Middle Kingdom hieratic handwriting had evolved different styles for different types of text. In particular, the careful literary hand was distinct from the more rapid hand used for administrative documents and letters. Thus, it is possible to identify the type of a text even from a fragment of papyrus with only one or two signs.

Few papyri survive from the Second Intermediate Period, but these have a sufficient range of genres to suggest that different types of text did not continue to be written in such distinctive styles. They include the literary Papyrus Westcar, the Rhind Mathematical Papyrus and fragments of a literary roll (BM EA 10475). Texts of the same period on other materials show the same unity of script across different types of document. These include a pair of writing boards with literary texts (the Carnarvon Tablets, now in the Egyptian Museum in Cairo), a mathematical leather roll and a group of ostraca with accountancy and some literary texts (from Deir el-Ballas). The handwriting of the period is distinctively rounded and curling and less angular than in the preceding dynasties.

In the New Kingdom, from the reign of Thutmes III, the forms of hieratic signs were systematically revised. This revision was marked by a return toward the hieroglyphs which underlay hieratic signs. The handwriting also appears swifter and more floridly calligraphic, although

13 *An example of a fine late New Kingdom hieratic hand. The roll is a record of an inspection of royal tombs on the West Bank at Thebes, including the robbed tomb of king Sekhemrashedtawy Sobekemsaf. The sheet-join (right over left) is clearly visible. Late Twentieth Dynasty, c.1100 BC, from Thebes. H. 42.5 cm. EA 10221.1.*

34

13 'calligraphy' does not seem to have existed as an art form distinct from fine handwriting. The writing styles did not again begin to diverge according to text type until later in the Eighteenth Dynasty. There seem to have been differences between styles in the north and the south, although these may sometimes be differences between individuals rather than regions. In the Third Intermediate Period, funerary texts were written in a most regular hieratic which seems to have been developed from the literary hands of the Ramesside Period.

By the Third Intermediate Period the form of script used for letters and accounts had become much more cursive; in the Theban area during this period it developed into a variant now known as 'abnormal hieratic'. Abnormal hieratic continued to be used there until the later sixth century BC, but in the seventh century BC the central government standardised the business hieratic of Lower Egypt into a new script for documents

14, 24, 29, 46, 56

which is now known as 'demotic' (meaning 'popular', as opposed to the less cursive hieratic that continued in use for religious documents). After its introduction in Lower Egypt demotic spread to Thebes when the Lower Egyptian Twenty-sixth Dynasty took control of southern Upper Egypt from the Sudanese kings of the Twenty-fifth Dynasty. The wealth of demotic documentation surpasses that of comparable earlier periods.

Early in the Roman Period the increasing use of Greek for all administrative affairs led to the death of demotic as a legal script. Demotic continued to be used for literary and religious texts; it seems to have been first used for sacred writings in the Ptolemaic Period. The Roman Period witnessed a movement towards a simpler and more mechanical style and demotic manuscripts began to die out in the third century AD (one of the last being a magical text BM EA 10070). The script lingered on in the far south, with the latest known demotic inscription at Philae dating to AD 452.

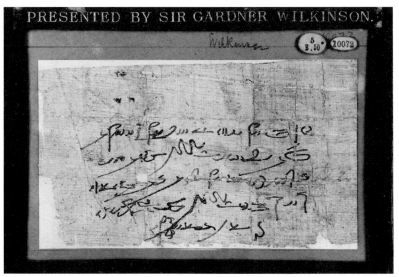

14 *An example of demotic handwriting on a small piece of papyrus used for a funerary text. Roman Period, second century AD, from Thebes. H. 9.5 cm. EA 10072.*

B/W 274259.

In scribal training, it seems that the most cursive script of the period was the first to be learnt, and for the majority of scribes the only one. This was because it was used for the most common types of text – documents and letters. In the second century AD Clement of Alexandria recorded that 'the men of learning among the Egyptians learnt first of all that method of writing called the epistolographic ['for writing letters', demotic], and second the hieratic, which the sacred scribes use, and then, last of all, the hieroglyphic'. From hieratic graffiti left on monuments by New Kingdom tourists it is clear that some scribes who could write hieratic had difficulties in reading the hieroglyphs. By contrast, Egyptologists find hieroglyphs easier than hieratic, being trained on hieroglyphs that are often typeset. Such hieroglyphs lack the cursive ligatures that have always been a possible source of misreadings, but which would have posed fewer problems to a practising scribe.

The modern reader of a papyrus faces the handiwork of a fallible individual, which often lacked the care spent on the fine inscriptions that had been drafted and carved by several hands. Some scribes, however, achieved results of the highest accuracy in hieratic and also of remarkable elegance, even in administrative and legal documents; in these, beauty and sense go hand in hand. Sometimes a copyist without a good reading knowledge could write a beautiful, but unintelligible, cursive text. The same phenomenon occurs in hieroglyphic texts, as on some coffins of the ninth century BC from Saqqara, where garbled signs fill the space where an illiterate craftsmen knew a text should be present. To modern eyes hieratic may look less neat than an inscription, but it was intended to be read for its sense, unlike some decorative inscriptions.

front cover

The features of the evolving hieratic style are often the only means of dating a manuscript, while the handwriting of different contemporaneous scribes can also be distinguished. Literary manuscripts from the Middle Kingdom onwards often had colophons, stating that the text was complete; the standard Middle Kingdom version affirms 'It is finished from beginning to end, as it was found in writing'. One Eighteenth Dynasty *Book of the Dead* adds 'having been copied revised, compared and verified sign by sign', but in general manuscripts provide little evidence for the practice of textual criticism. Occasionally the colophon gave details of the scribe and a name can be put to the handwriting: there are several fine manuscripts written by one Inene, a treasury official of Sety II (for example BM EA 10182), and the hand of the learned scribe Qenherkhopshef from Deir el-Medina is instantly recognisable, being very swift and untidily sprawling. In a Ramesside literary letter one scribe boasts to a rival that he is 'one who hastens to cover empty sheets' (BM EA 10247), and a frequent claim was to be 'excellent of fingers'. This assertion can sometimes be supplemented or qualified by the actual results: the Twelfth Dynasty scribe Amenaa, who copied out the *Tale of the Shipwrecked Sailor* (now in the Hermitage, St Petersburg), made this claim in his colophon, and his copy is fine but not perfect, containing a few slips.

9,15, 42, 43

42, 61

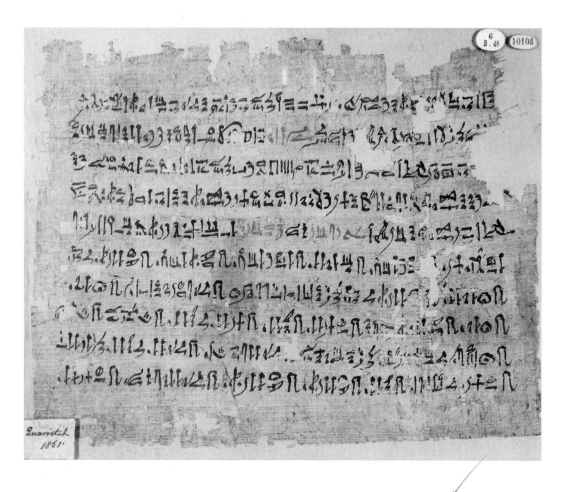

EQUIPMENT FOR WRITING

Writing tools are described in use in the Middle Kingdom *Words of Neferti*, where a sage recites a prophecy, and King Sneferu himself plays the scribe:

> *Then the King stretched out his hand to a box of writing equipment.*
> *Then he took for himself a roll and a palette.*
> *And he was writing down*
> *what the lector priest Neferti said.*

A late New Kingdom letter from Deir el-Medina provides a less courtly view, instructing its recipient:

> *Hurry to the magazine of Nefery and get the papyrus that is there together with the small scribal palette and send them to me! And open the little chest which is kept in the sitting room of the Gateway, and get the texts ... and attach them to a writing board [of gesso] together with some ... and send me some accounts of ...*

A depiction of the basic equipment used by the scribes (in Egyptian

15 *The last page of a series of incantations in hieratic, with instructions for use; at the end is a long colophon beginning 'it has come to a perfect close in peace ...'. The start of the instructions and the colophon are in red, but the word 'perfect' is in black to avoid the baleful colour red. Nineteenth Dynasty, c.1250 BC, provenance unknown. H. 19.2 cm. EA 10105.*

16 *(Above) A detailed version of the hieroglyph sesh, 'write', from the tomb-chapel of Iry, showing a rectangular palette with two wells for pigment, a circular container, and a cylindrical pen-case. Fifth Dynasty, c.2500 BC, from Saqqara. H. of sign 6.4 cm. EA 1168, detail of limestone relief.*

17 *(Right) Two palettes with hollows for pigment cakes and central grooves for reed pens. The narrow palette has two hollows for the black and red pigment, while the broad one has twelve more for other colours for illustrations. One of the reed pens still has red pigment at the tip. Early Eighteenth Dynasty, provenance unknown, c.1550 BC, H. 28.7 cm, EA 12784; c.1450 BC, H. 33.2 cm, EA 5512.*

menhed) was used as the hieroglyph for 'writing' and 'painting'. This sign **16** shows a holder for reed pens (*'ar*) in the shape of a palm column, a leather bag for pigment-pellets and sundries, and a small palette (*gesti*) with pigment (*riyt*), tied together. Early examples, on which the hieroglyph was based, consisted of a small tablet with two hollows to take the red and black pigments. The more common later scribal palettes were slender **17** strips of wood, from 20 to 43 cm long, 5 to 8 cm across and about 1.5 cm thick; some royal examples from the tomb of Tutankhamen were of ivory. Palettes are shown with cords attached at the top (to attach them to other equipment and to hang them over the shoulder). At one end shallow hollows were cut for the pigments and there was generally a central slot to hold some reeds. Painters' palettes were similar but broader, to accommodate a greater number of colours.

The equipment features in the Pyramid Texts, where the dead king threatens the gods' secretary (in order to secure his afterlife):

> *I shall smash your equipment*
> *I shall break your two pens*
> *I shall tear up your rolls.*

The 'two pens' probably reflect a regular use of one pen for black pigment and a different one for red, the two principal colours. This is born out by the fact that red signs on manuscripts show no contaminating traces of black. Scribes were often portrayed with several pens; for example, one in the hand and two tucked behind the ear. These pens were made from rushes (1.5–2.5 mm in diameter) and were thicker than the Greek-style reed pen adopted at the end of the Ptolemaic Period. These were split, unlike the rush pens, and they allowed cursive signs to be written at a smaller scale. Pens were around 20 cm long and representations show that a scribe held his pen *c.* 3–6 cm from the end, with the hand clear of the surface to avoid smudging while writing from right to left. The rush pen had no ink reservoirs (and the palette had no wells); the pen was wetted in a water-vessel and then the damp pen was rubbed on an ink cake to fill it with ink. Without frequent refilling, this practice produced a rapid change from dark to pale ink when writing, but this does not seem to have been considered a fault to be avoided; in some manuscripts a single dipping writes only five or six signs. Considerable experience was needed to use a rush pen well. Although pen-strokes were less fine, the rush pen did have some advantages over the reed pen: there was no need, for example, to keep resharpening it and it wrote more easily on a flexible surface. A reed pen was sharper and its use involved greater pressure on the writing surface (it is noticeable that when the reed pen was adopted, manufactured papyrus became thicker). A rush pen cannot draw a stroke from bottom right to top left, and in general movement from right to left is slightly awkward. This accounted for much of the abbreviation of signs in the cursive scripts, such as the completion of only the left half of some signs.

The scribe's tools were not restricted to this very portable assemblage and a range is shown on the iconographic 'friezes of objects' painted inside Middle Kingdom coffins, where it is termed *kh'aw nu sekh* 'equipment for writing'. These included cases for documents and equipment, of oval shape rather like a satchel (*seheter* or more commonly just *kheret-'a*, 'writing materials'). Another type of document case was cylindrical

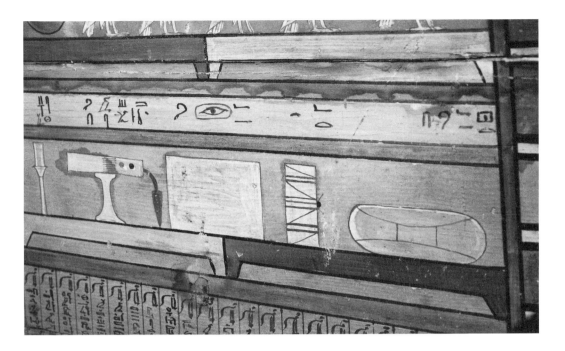

18 *Writing equipment, as depicted on the outer coffin of the physician Gua; the name and number of each item is written in hieratic. The objects are (right to left): 'writing board container – 110', 'roll', 'writing board – 100', and 'palette and water pot – 110'. Mid-Twelfth Dynasty, c.1850 BC, from el-Bersha. H. of band of objects 9 cm. EA 30839, detail.*

(rather like a duffle bag) and made of basketwork with a flexible (perhaps leather) top that could be tied shut. Other necessities were a water pot (*pas*), a shell to contain pigment (*wedj'ayt*), papyrus rolls (sometimes shown standing on their ends, tied together in a bundle) and writing boards ('*an*). There were separate words for a papyrus (*shefdu*), a roll of any material ('*aret*) and a written book or document (*medjat*). As well as these, the equipment included a grinder for preparing pigment, a stone (perhaps to smooth or pound papyrus) and an instrument shaped like a small mallet that is usually considered to be for smoothing the surface or sheet-joins ('burnishers'). An elaborate ivory example survives from the tomb of Tutankhamen, but John Tait notes that it was too flimsy to have been pushed with any great pressure over a surface. (If they were not used for smoothing or pounding, they might have been used for some action such as holding unrolled papyrus flat.) Other representations show that scribes were often provided with low flat wooden chests, used as document-boxes.

The most complete surviving set of equipment is a working example from a burial at Thebes. It was discovered by Howard Carter in a rushwork basket among the mixed grave goods of fourteen coffins piled up during the Second Intermediate Period and early Eighteenth Dynasty in a Middle Kingdom tomb chamber. When opened, the basket revealed the following items:

> 1. *A case formed from the stem of a thick rush in the shape of a palm column. This case contained twenty-six thin reeds for use as pens, and a few seeds of unknown purpose, probably there by chance.*

20, 36

19

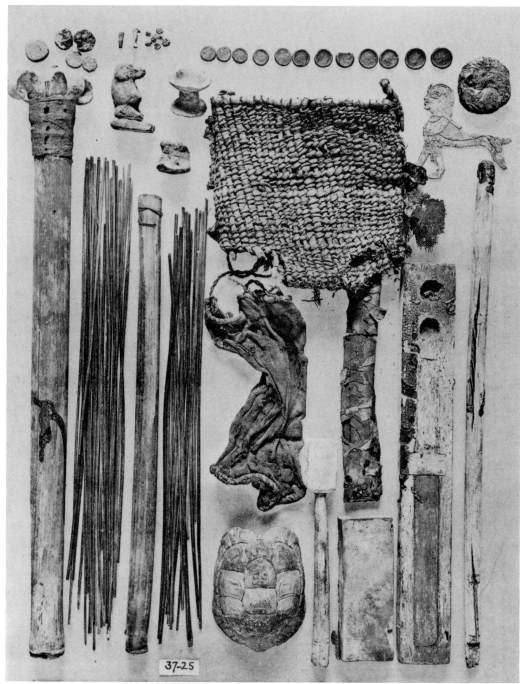

B/W 273094

19   *The set of writing equipment discovered by Howard Carter among Second Intermediate Period and early Eighteenth Dynasty burials in a tomb next to the Hatshepsut temple causeway on the West Bank at Thebes. Early Eighteenth Dynasty, c.1500 BC.*

2. *A smaller and plainer case, holding fifteen reeds and some more seeds.*
3. *A scribal palette of wood, with two circular depressions for black and red pigment.*
4. *A wooden 'burnisher' (see above).*
5. *A slab of hard wood with two holes at one side and a third at one end, all containing broken pegs; this was presumably a board to work on.*
6. *A stick 30 cm long, perhaps the cross-bar of a pair of scales.*
7. *A small string bag.*
8. *A linen purse with string cord.*
9. *A leather roll, tied up with linen.*
10. *A roll of linen.*
11. *Scraps from a papyrus roll.*
12. *One large and several small lumps of wax, resin, and unidentified matter.*
13. *A tortoise-shell, presumably a container for water or pigment.*
14. *A clay ball, and another lump of clay shaped like a knucklebone (possibly weights).*
15. *A clay miniature cup, perhaps for making an offering.*
16. *A clay figurine of Thoth as a baboon.*
17. *A green glazed composition figurine, apparently in the form of a mummy.*
18. *A sheet copper image of a standing sphinx.*

Some of these items remain enigmatic, but they must have provided the scribe in his office with the materials for his job (which would include weighing and recording figures). The figurine of Thoth suggests that offering incense to the god of writing was part of the scribe's working day. The resinous and other materials may have been connected with this, or with the preparation of pigments.

A less extensive writing set, wrapped in two long strips of linen, was discovered by the New York Metropolitan Museum of Art expedition of 1912–13 in a reused Middle Kingdom tomb at Thebes. This consisted of a wooden palette (26 x 4 cm), with a slot at the centre to hold one rather worn old pen and three new ones, all made of slender reeds (only 3 mm in diameter). Two sheets of papyrus were tied to the palette, both 23.5 cm high, one 91 cm wide and the other 27.7 cm wide. The larger sheet bore traces of an erased administrative account in a hieratic hand that points to a date in the late Eighteenth or early Nineteenth Dynasty. A ball of linen thread was tucked in with the papyri and palette; this was obviously used to tie up rolls. The names of the owners of these sets have not survived.

Scribes are usually shown squatting or cross-legged, with the papyrus on their lap, and apparently no other support than the roll itself and the tautly stretched cloth of their kilts. In relief and paintings, however, they are also shown standing and writing on what seems to be a board held at an angle in their left hand, or squatting and writing on a board leant against their document case or box. They are surrounded by various

21, 22, III

20

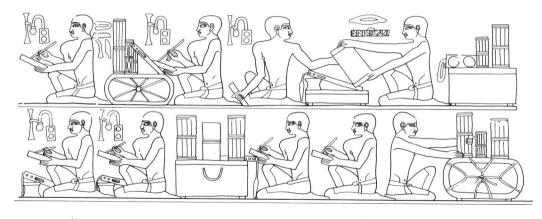

20 *(Above) Detail of the scene of 'assessment by the board of the estate', showing scribes writing, while one takes a roll from the 'keeper of the rolls', and another moves a bound stack of rolls; the papyri are stored in chests and oval containers. Limestone relief in the tomb-chapel of Ti, at Saqqara (after a drawing by Henri Wild). Fifth Dynasty, c.2400 BC.*

pieces of equipment and tied up bundles of rolls. Another position depicted is that of sitting on stools, writing on their laps with a chest at their sides, as can be seen in one representation of a records office; when in well appointed government offices, senior scribes may not always have squatted on the ground. Occasionally, short notes have been found jotted on the scribal palette itself instead of a board and some representations of standing scribes seem to show the palette being written on or used as a support for another writing surface.

The squatting writing posture was immortalised in the form of the scribal statue, which is attested from all the principal periods of Egyptian art. In the Old Kingdom scribal statues were placed in the tomb with other images of the deceased. Later, they were found only in temples and the scribe's roll was then often inscribed with a religious text. Wooden models of daily life were placed in tombs of the late Old and early Middle Kingdom; here the scribal figures squat with small rolls or, more often, wooden tablets upon which accounts have been added for realistic effect.

41

VII

22

23

21 *(Left) Scribes in the administration, seated on the ground and writing on papyrus rolls stretched across their laps. Detail of limestone relief in the tomb of the general (later king) Horemheb, at Saqqara. Late Eighteenth Dynasty, c.1300 BC.*

22 (Above) Views from the front and from above of a quartzite statue of the scribe Pesshuper. A papyrus roll lies across his lap, and his right hand is poised as if holding a reed pen. A shell-shaped palette is on his left knee, while another palette slung over his left shoulder acts as a sign of his profession. Twenty-sixth Dynasty, c.600 BC, from Thebes. H. 53 cm. EA 1514.

23 (Right) This wooden model shows a scribe sitting on the upper level of a granary, recording quantities of grain on a white wooden writing-board. Early Middle Kingdom, c.2000 BC, from Beni Hasan. H. of scribe 12.5 cm. EA 41573.

In front of some is a chest with a scribal palette laid out on top. Often the palette was put elsewhere while writing, as a description of scribes in the Coffin Texts shows: 'with the texts on their thighs and the palette in their armpit'. With one or two exceptions all representations of scribes show them as right-handed.

Laying out a Document

No less than a modern writer, the Egyptian scribe laid out what he wrote on his sheet in different ways according to the type of text. New Kingdom *Book of the Dead* papyri, for example, followed the same rules of decorum as monumental texts and reliefs: the text was arranged in columns separated by lines, in an area surrounded by a coloured border. In the roll belonging to the official Ani the painted borders had evidently been drawn (though not coloured) before the full roll was assembled, since they do not always join up neatly at the sheet joins. With cursive hieroglyphs, ruled lines and borders usually separated columns or framed sections, but for hieratic such elaborations were dispensed with.

10, 25, 36, 51, V, VI

When starting to write hieratic, the scribe would undo the roll on his lap, with the short end on his right side, and begin his text on the recto. One exception to this procedure occurs in late New Kingdom letters and documents, where the text seems to have been begun on the verso. For these the scribe had in fact placed the roll on his lap with the short end at the top (that is, sideways), making the text start on fibres running perpendicular not parallel to the text. It is not obvious why this was done.

At the start of the roll a margin was left, to protect the text once it was rolled up; sometimes a strengthening strip was added, which was often cut from a reused roll (for example, the demotic document BM EA 10380, which is strengthened with a strip of the owner's marriage contract). These strips vary between 5 and 9 cm in width and were occasionally added to both ends of a roll. Vertical lines of hieratic would then be written continuously from right to left; horizontal lines would be written in columns or 'pages', no longer than the amount of roll that a scribe could unroll on his lap (the pages did not necessarily follow the sheets of the roll, though some scribes tried to avoid writing over the thick sheet joins). The pages were laid out freehand, aided slightly by the papyrus fibres and the vertical lines of the sheet joins. At the top and bottom, margins of a few centimetres were left, to protect the text from the inevitable fraying of the edges of the roll. Care was usually taken to keep the right-hand edge of each page straight, but the left is often slightly ragged; the gaps between the pages vary in width from 1.5 to 3 cm, and occasionally a vertical drawn line had to be added when the pages ran into each other. The number of lines in each page of a roll also varied slightly. Horizontal lines of text tended to be more swiftly written than vertical lines, and to be less legible, with more ligatures; they could fit more words onto the papyrus. Another advantage of horizontal writing is that, while the hand conceals the previous lines when writing vertically from right to left, it does not conceal the preceding lines when writing horizontally. Vertical lines, which used the space less economically, were more frequently employed in prestigious or archaistic manuscripts.

24

5

13, 15, 42, 46, 61

In the Old Kingdom, when the use of writing was less widespread, hieratic texts were almost always in vertical lines. The Middle Kingdom witnessed a gradual shift from vertical to horizontal: at the start of the

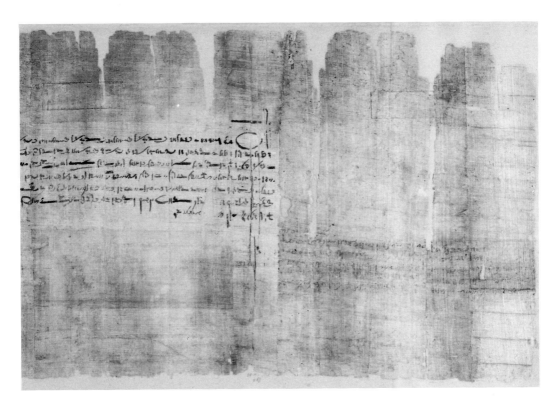

24 *A strengthening strip on a demotic papyrus. A man called Pasherpamut used a broad strip torn from an erased roll to reinforce another document, then at least six years old; the still legible traces on the strip show that he had torn up his marriage contract. Ptolemaic Period, 231 BC (main document) and 225–4 BC (strip), from Thebes. H. 33.5 cm. EA 10380, detail.*

forty-six-year reign of Amenemhat III, personal letters were written in vertical lines, but by its end they were generally written in horizontal lines. An introductory vertical line was kept as a formatting convention and sometimes a closing line or two was also written vertically. Middle Kingdom literary manuscripts often begin and end in vertical lines, while the central portion of the work is horizontal. This manner of presentation survived into the Second Intermediate Period, as in the Rhind Mathematical Papyrus where the mathematical examples are in horizontal lines but are preceded by four vertical lines of introduction (BM EA 10057/8). In the New Kingdom hieratic was invariably horizontal, while the more formal cursive hieroglyphs remained largely vertical. Demotic is always in horizontal lines.

In the Middle Kingdom, upper and lower margin lines are sometimes found in literary papyri (perhaps to help keep the margins even), but vertical margin lines are much rarer. One small literary fragment from Lahun (late Middle Kingdom) has margin lines at the vertical and horizontal edges of the text. Its sixth vertical column has the number 6 written below the bottom margin line. Such column-numbering is very rare (another Middle Kingdom example is BM EA 10274). Pages were also numbered very occasionally (for example, BM EA 9913 from the Eighteenth Dynasty), as were lines in lists. In the Roman Period guidelines for each line of text appear in both hieratic and demotic manuscripts, as part of a general tendency towards a more mechanical style of writing.

27

34

25

B/w 273840.

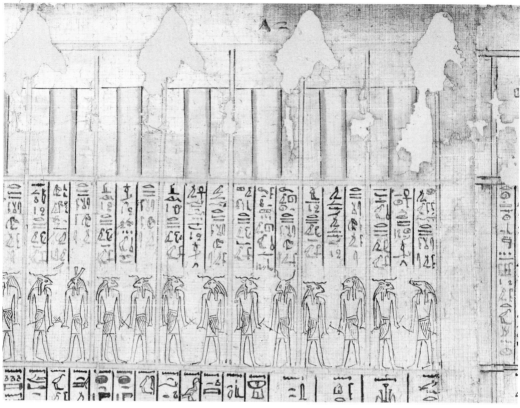

When a scribe ran out of room on a roll, he would either paste on extra sheets or turn the roll over (usually on a vertical axis, according to Jaroslav Černý) and continue writing on the verso. Before the Middle Kingdom, scribes seem to have been disinclined to use the verso.

7, 26   Variation in layout according to the type of text can be seen most clearly in administrative documents, where information is presented not in a single stream of text in continuous lines but in tabulated form. In the Old Kingdom accounts documents were often tabulated within grids, as in temple inventories or records of work arranged day by day. Although the layout could be extremely careful, sometimes the entries in each square or rectangle of the table were written with little regard for the framing lines. After the Old Kingdom detailed grids are rare but horizontal guidelines at regular intervals of three lines of text remain common in types of text that involved extensive tabulation, but even these reduced guides to spacing are rare after the beginning of the Eighteenth Dynasty

34   (one of the latest examples being the Rhind Mathematical Papyrus).

There is a variety of conventions for particular document types. Items in inventories and lists were laid out on separate horizontal lines, even when they were a part of a continuous text. The final signs of words (the 'determinatives' which indicate the type of object meant) were arranged into a distinct column. Legal and accounts documents used abbreviations

25 *A rare example of page-numbering on a papyrus roll (top, centre) from the* Book of the Dead *of a man named Tui. The numbers are in hieratic, and very unusually read from left to right, following the direction of the cursive hieroglyphic script below. Early Eighteenth Dynasty, c.1450 BC, provenance unknown. EA 9913, detail.*

26 *A part of a darkened roll containing the records of timber work at the royal dockyards of Memphis under Prince Amenhotep. The narrow columns of accounts are separated by short blank spaces. Note the broad sheet-join on the right (left over right, although the text reads from right to left). Early Eighteenth Dynasty, c.1425 BC, probably from Saqqara. H. 16.8 cm. EA 10056, detail.*

as well as small dashes of red or black that functioned as checkmarks. In a duty roster these checkmarks could indicate service on a particular day; in a list of workers dashes marked an individual's presence or absence at the start of work. Accounts documents often used small dashes as ditto-marks, but a phrase could also be repeated by leaving blank the space below the part of line to be repeated, or by writing a phrase common to a group of horizontal lines in the margin alongside them. Literary manuscripts occasionally used blanks instead of ditto-marks to indicate a repeated phrase such as a refrain. When a sentence was to be repeated with one varying phrase, the sentence was written once, but the column was split into two sub-columns for the two different phrases.

Letters had various distinctive features. Royal letters or decrees were sometimes inscribed on tomb-chapel walls or as temple stelae, following the format of the papyrus original. Some originals have been recovered from the archive of the Old Kingdom king Raneferef at Abusir, by the Czechoslovak expedition in 1979. The decrees were arranged in a careful combination of vertical and horizontal lines, with the message in vertical lines under a horizontal heading ('Royal Decree'). A vertical heading at the start gave the royal name and date. Private letters had a less elaborate layout, but were still distinctive. In the Middle Kingdom, for example, the epistolary greetings that opened all letters were occasionally written in a large florid style (for example, BM EA 10567).

A letter occupied a sheet rather than a roll of papyrus, and was simply

27

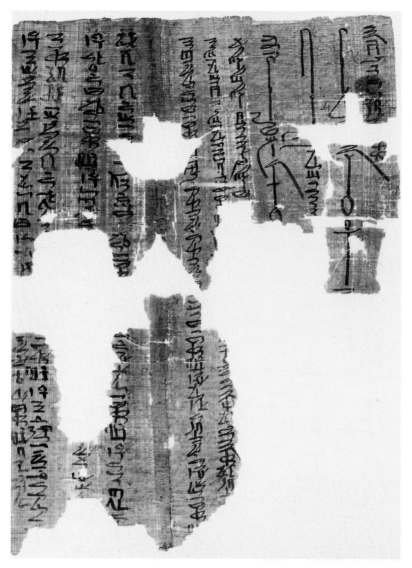

27 *Letter from a man named Sankhenra; the scribe took the first part of a letter, containing introductory formulae, changed the name (see fig. 32) and pasted to the left another (reused) sheet on which he then wrote the new message. The join can be seen at the centre. Early Middle Kingdom, c.2000 BC, from Thebes. H. 30 cm. EA 10567.*

cut or torn from an existing roll. Letters were hardly ever longer than one sheet and a short message might be written on a small scrap; one late New Kingdom message is a mere 11.5 × 6.5 cm (BM EA 10101). Even a full letter might be quite small: an early Eighteenth Dynasty example from Ptahu to the scribe Ahmes of Peniaty measures 14 × 8.8 cm (BM EA 10107). Letters were not rolled like other manuscripts but were folded into small packets to be carried. The address was then written on the outside in a vertical line, with the name of sender and courier, and sometimes a date, on the other side of the package, usually in horizontal lines. The packet was tied with string or a wisp of papyrus and fastened, sometimes simply with an object that happened to be at hand, such as the fishhook that sealed one Middle Kingdom letter from Lahun. More often

28

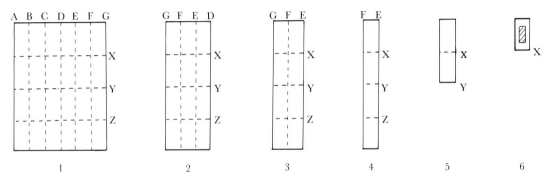

A B C D E F G	G F E D	G F E	F E		
X	X	X	X	X	X
Y	Y	Y	Y	Y	
Z	Z	Z	Z		
1	2	3	4	5	6

28 *The way in which an early Middle Kingdom letter (EA 10549) was folded, reconstructed from the crease-marks on the papyrus sheet. H. 26 cm (unfolded).*

the tie of the string was sealed with a small piece of Nile mud bearing the imprint of a stamp seal.

Seals were probably applied to many rolls and would have been particularly important for some categories of official or legal documents. Some small demotic records of loans, for example, have a summary at the top, which was folded over and sealed, so that if the main text was surreptitiously altered, any attempt on this could be detected by the broken seal. On some, the seals were still intact when they were discovered (for example, BM EA 10831). **29**

29 *(Right) Papyrus sheet bearing the text of a loan in demotic. A résumé of the details was written at the top, and was separately tied with a papyrus fibre and sealed, so that it could be checked if the main text was altered. Ptolemaic Period, 194 BC, from Thebes. H. 23 cm. EA 10831.*

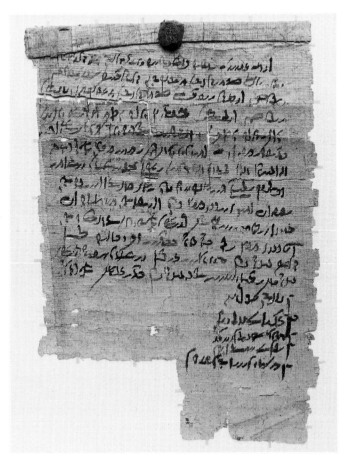

30 *Part of a papyrus roll with two columns of the* Teaching of Amenemope. *Each 'stanza' is labelled and numbered in red (here the 'fifth' and 'sixth stanza'), and each verse is placed on a separate line. Third Intermediate Period, c.1000 BC, provenance unknown. H. 24 cm.* EA *10474.2, detail.*

Texts were generally written continuously, and words could be split between lines, although not all scribes adopted this practice. Headings and dates, however, were often set apart on a separate line, and stichic writing was used in accounts for tabulation and for lists. In Middle Kingdom literary texts short sections or stanzas were occasionally written on separate lines: examples include hymns with refrains from Lahun and a set of maxims (Papyrus Ramesseum 2, now BM EA 10755). The ends of lines of verse were indicated with punctuation (see below), though in one Third Intermediate Period copy of the *Teaching of Amenemope* each line of verse was written on a separate line (BM EA 10474). This became usual in demotic wisdom texts but in the demotic *Song of the Harper* and in a late religious text (BM EA 10507), each line seems to contain two verses. This tendency not to distinguish verse from prose in writing is far from unique.

INK AND PUNCTUATION

In most periods, the two principal pigments were black and red. Black ink was invariably from carbon and red ink was usually haematite (a naturally occurring iron oxide). The ground pigment was made into small cakes with a binding medium, and each cake was stored in a small circular depression in the scribal palette. Religious texts and spells sometimes specify that the text should be written with *antyu*, an aromatic substance much used in cult and probably similar to gum arabic; one Eighteenth Dynasty scribal statue of the head craftsman Teti (from Deir el-Bahri, now in the National Museums of Scotland, Edinburgh) has the

31 *Part of a papyrus roll with a guide to the 'good' or 'bad' nature of consecutive days. The dates and the signs for 'bad' are written in red, the rest in black. In the upper margin the scribe has rewritten certain signs. Late Nineteenth Dynasty, c.1225 BC, from Saqqara. H. 19.5 cm. EA 10184.4.*

word *antyu* carved in one of the two depressions in the scribal palette. This substance may have been used only for the most sacred texts.

While black was the main ink, red ink was a practical means of highlighting phrases ('rubrics') and marking distinctions. For example, the totals in accounts were put in red, as were certain words such as 'emmer', to distinguish them for other grain notations. Different types of texts highlight different types of phrases: in medical and magical papyri the quantities of ingredients for potions were rubricised, or whole sections describing how to perform a spell were written in red; in religious texts red was used for the names of demons, as it was symbolically a colour of ill-omen (the desert was the 'red land'). Red could simply mark a reply added to a letter, or insertions and corrections to a copied text. Perhaps the most widespread use of red was to indicate headings and the opening phrases of a section of a text. Thus the dates at the head of administrative texts were usually rubricised, with one exception: the word for 'year' remained in black, since the ill-omened red was inappropriate for a king's name or regnal year. In literary hieratic the first verse of a stanza was a rubric, although these rubrics were marked more consistently in horizontal rather than vertical lines.

Red ink was no longer used in demotic papyri of the Ptolemaic Period, although it continued to occur in religious manuscripts written in hieratic and hieroglyphs. Later, red is used in demotic religious documents. Without red ink, demotic literary texts sometimes marked the start of sections with a new line, like modern paragraphs.

In Egyptian scripts no space was left between words although the

IV

31, 43, V

30

hieroglyphic system assisted the reader to determine their ends, usually by marking them with meaning signs ('determinatives'). This feature must have made reading easier in general, although it did not help the reader to recognise the ends of phrases, which were unmarked. The need for punctuation was obviously not felt, perhaps in part due to the paucity of very long texts and the fact that reading was a specialised activity, and was probably never very fast.

The royal funerary inscriptions of the Old Kingdom, the Pyramid Texts, and their successors, the non-royal Coffin Texts of the Middle Kingdom, show features which may have been found on contemporaneous papyri. In the Pyramid Texts, lines at the end of a section were sometimes added to turn the column into a *hut*-hieroglyph enclosing the whole section: ⌷ . *Hut* ('mansion') denotes a 'section' or (by the similar modern metaphor) 'stanza'. On coffins, a red line occasionally marked the end of short sections of spells; this may have derived from tabulated columns in accounts on papyri or from the Pyramid Texts. Red lines were not restricted to coffins; one such example occurs on a fragment of papyrus from Lahun, bearing the ritual of offering a meal to Osiris in vertical lines of cursive hieroglyphs. The lines are also known from the cursive copies that New Kingdom scribes made of an old didactic text known as *Kemyt*; here they marked the ends of short phrases which apparently correspond to lines of verse or units for recitation.

By the New Kingdom, a slightly different system of punctuation had been developed for literary texts which was more suitable for hieratic written in horizontal lines. This consisted of red points placed just above the line ('verse points'), which were apparently added after a section of text had been written (and were consequently often misplaced). They appear first in Middle Kingdom papyri, from both the south and the north (examples being Papyrus Ramesseum 2 from Thebes and some literary fragments from Lahun, now in University College London), but become widespread only in the New Kingdom; they survive in a few demotic manuscripts. Verse points were used for types of text where recitation was important and, while they must have aided scanning a text, their inconsistent usage shows that this was possible without them. They may have been introduced as scansion became more of an acquired skill and less of a natural part of reading, as the spoken language evolved away from the literary language and its metrical forms. As part of this system, a specific sign for the end of a stanza was applied, which seems to be an abbreviation for the word 'pause' (*gereh*): ⌒ . The shape may have been adopted in imitation of *hut*-markers that are found in some Pyramid Texts, although any direct connection between the papyri and these inscriptions is unlikely (lost manuscripts of temple ritual may have been the link).

9, 61, IV

61

Errors, Erasures and Reuse

As in any piece of handwriting, errors occur occasionally on papyrus. One feature of many copies is a deterioration and hastiness as the scribe's concentration faded towards the end of a document or a copying session. Apprentice scribes often marked the end of a session with the day's date, which makes it easier to detect such failings. A survey of variants and errors suggests that apprentices mostly wrote from copies and not from dictation. Some New Kingdom copies of earlier literary texts were so garbled as to be almost incomprehensible; this applies especially to texts such as the *Teaching of Khety*, which praised the profession of the scribe (e.g. BM EA 10182). This was probably due not to the copyist but to the fact that he had a bad original to copy, the text having been corrupted by its transmission over the centuries since its composition in the Twelfth Dynasty.

Different scribes tended to make different types of errors, such as consistent misspellings. In some New Kingdom literary copies, signs are written above the text and have been interpreted as corrections by a master scribe. Sometimes, however, these appear to be in the same hand, as if the copyist himself occasionally rewrote a sign for his own instruction. Elsewhere, corrections are distinctly marked by crossings out (sometimes in red), either by the copyist or by a second hand. Omitted words or phrases could be added immediately above the line, if there was enough room; if not, the scribe would mark the place of omission with a cross and write the omitted words in the margin. Sometimes one can see a sign half finished as the scribe realised his mistake and then wrote the correct sign half over it, without bothering to finish or erase the mistake; this is a habit of the Twelfth Dynasty scribe of a copy of the *Tale of the Eloquent Peasant* (now in the Egyptian Museum, Berlin).

Drastic erasures could cover entire sheets and even rolls, but this was for the sake of reuse, not correction. Palimpsest, a Greek term meaning 'rubbed again', is used to describe a manuscript that has been cleaned and smoothed for reuse. The Gebelein Papyri date to the Fourth Dynasty and are the oldest surviving written papyri; two out of five of these are palimpsest. Such levels of reuse seem to have been the norm in most periods. The process of erasure must have involved more than merely water, as papyrus can be soaked without washing out the ink, even though the surface is very non-absorbent. One possible method would be with water and light rubbing, and from the determinative with which a word 'to erase' (*fetet* 🖐) is written, licking has been suggested as a way to erase single words. This procedure can perhaps be seen in one Middle Kingdom letter (BM EA 10567), whose text was reused after the old address was erased and a new one substituted: there is still a clear smudge. In one Twelfth Dynasty literary manuscript (the *Tale of Sinuhe*, now in the Egyptian Museum, Berlin), the scribe was not satisfied with his erasure and seems to have simply cut out the mistaken line and patched the roll together again. There was probably no need for any solvent, although a third- to fourth-century AD Greek chemical text preserves a recipe for a paste to whiten pearls which could also be 'used for palimpsesting written papyrus rolls'.

31, 61

32

32 *Detail of the first line of a letter (see fig. 27), showing the thumbprint left by the scribe as he reused an old letter; he smudged out the name of the original addressee and replaced it, without rewriting the introductory greetings. Early Middle Kingdom, c.2000 BC, from Thebes. EA 10567, detail.*

Although a whole text could be wiped off to make way for a new text to be written, reuse did not always require washing: often the first use of a roll left the verso blank and this could be used for another later text. However, some rolls with an empty verso were nevertheless palimpsested. A new text could be inserted in the spaces left empty by the first text: such jottings and notes are common. Practical considerations that now cannot be reconstructed will have determined the procedures for reuse. One New Kingdom literary papyrus (Papyrus Sallier 4, now BM EA 10184) was used and abused over several decades; some doodles and jottings on the verso were written not only upside down but also across the roll, while 7.5 m of text were erased from the recto. Full-height papyri with chancellery documents were often halved and reused, as in the case of Papyrus Petersburg 1116a (now in the Hermitage, St Petersburg), in which the scribe Khaemwaset split a set of accounts and copied the *Teaching for Merikare* onto the verso of the bottom half. The faint traces of an earlier text under the reuse are always tantalising, but usually illegible, even with the help of infrared photography.

New papyri tended to be reserved for prestigious documents, and one Middle Kingdom author (the hero of the *Tale of the Eloquent Peasant*) is favoured by having his rhetoric copied at court onto a 'new roll'. New rolls are most commonly found with state texts or with religious and funerary literature, which often referred to the use of fresh papyrus. In the *Book of the Dead*, one spell was 'to be put in writing on a new sheet of papyrus and placed under the head' of the mummy. However, even *Books of the Dead* include examples of palimpsest, for example the tenth-century papyrus of Buhar (BM EA 9974). This roll was laid out for a text but this was not completely written and the vignette now stands out against an obviously palimpsest sheet with traces of some erased accounts.

Some gaps in manuscripts are not due to erasure: the copyist occasionally had to leave a word blank because it had been illegibly written in his original, was lost in a lacuna or needed checking and was intended to be filled in later. Religious texts copied from venerable originals often leave spaces empty to indicate lacunae, or have the frank comment *gem-wesh*, 'found lacking', or more rarely *shu em-iry-ef*, 'empty of what belongs there'.

33 *Papyrus roll with a vignette of a man offering to a falcon-headed god on the first sheet; on the following sheets, intended for chapters of the* Book of the Dead *in hieratic, there are traces of an erased grain account. Note the two sheet-joins. Third Intermediate Period, c.950 BC, from Thebes.* H. 11.8 cm. EA 9974.

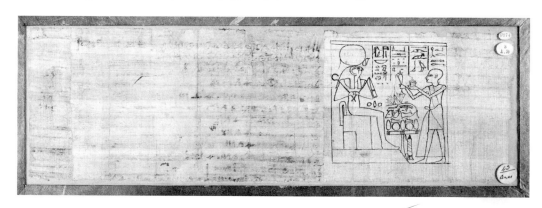

I *Papyrus marshes near Syracuse, in Sicily. Courtesy of W. V. Davies.*

II *A wall-painting showing birds in a papyrus thicket. Watercolour copy by Nina de Garis Davies, in the Department of Egyptian Antiquities, the British Museum, from a late Eighteenth Dynasty original, c.1350 BC; painted plaster, from Amarna. H. of bird 19 cm.*

III *A wall-painting showing scribes recording quantities of grain at harvest-time. Note the black pigment at the tips of their pens. Watercolour copy by Nina de Garis Davies, in the Department of Egyptian Antiquities, the British Museum, from mid-Eighteenth Dynasty original, c.1400 BC; painted plaster, Thebes. H. of scribe on right (in original) 18 cm.*

IV *The start of a fragmentary papyrus roll containing a series of incantations. The words to be recited are written in black, the titles and instructions for each text in red. It is marked with 'versepoints' in red, overlaid in black when the text is in red. Nineteenth Dynasty, c.1250 BC, from Thebes. H. 21.5 cm. EA 9997.1, detail.*

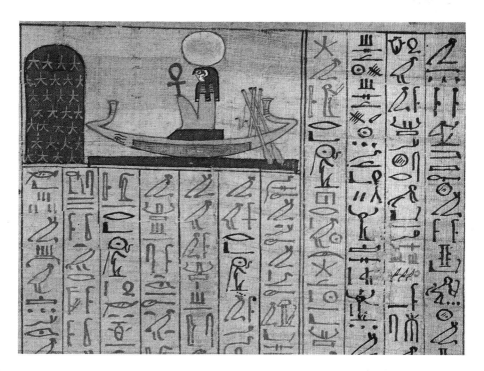

V *Detail from the* Book of the Dead *of Ani, written in cursive hieroglyphs. The illustration shows the sun-god Ra in his boat. The main text is in black, with titles and instructions in red. The name of Ra is in black, avoiding the baneful colour red, while the name of his enemy, Aapep, is in red (and cut with knives). Nineteenth Dynasty, c.1250 BC, from Thebes.* W. *of vignette 12.5 cm.* EA *10470.22, detail.*

VI *Final section of the* Book of the Dead *of Amenhotep, the overseer of builders of the god Amun, written in retrograde cursive hieroglyphs. The green pigment in the illustration has eaten through the papyrus. The vertical dark line is the right edge of a sheet-join. Early Eighteenth Dynasty, c.1450 BC, from Thebes.* H. *34 cm.* EA *10489.16.*

VII *A detail from the illustrated* Book of the Dead *of the King's Mother Nedjmet, showing her judgment after death. She bows before the god Thoth, who is represented as a baboon wearing the lunar crescent and disk, and writing the verdict onto his palette. Twenty-first Dynasty, c.1050 BC, from Thebes.* H. *of baboon on pedestal 7.5 cm.* EA *10541.*

VIII *Fragments of an illustrated papyrus, showing a god next to a temple pylon, a jackal-headed deity beside another pylon, and a woman before the god Inheret. As these motifs cannot be paralleled in funerary texts, the fragments may be from non-funerary manuscripts. Nineteenth Dynasty, c.1250 BC (?), from Thebes.* H. *of largest fragment 38 cm.* EA *9930 and 9931.*

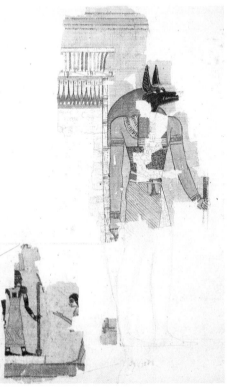
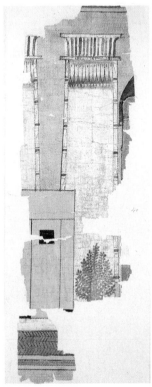

CHAPTER THREE

Contents and Storage

Look, their words endure in writings.
Open and read,
and emulate the wise!
Teaching for Merikare *(ed. Helck), 10c-d*

ATTITUDES TO WRITING

The surviving Pharaonic evidence is insufficient to estimate precisely what percentage of the population was literate, in the sense of being able either to read and write with fluency or merely to write their name for daily affairs. Nevertheless it is significant that attempts to calculate the rate of full literacy produce figures of between 0.3 and 5 per cent, with the figure rising through Egyptian history. Writing and reading were exclusively elite affairs, confined to the ruling stratum of society and its secretaries. There was a marginal extension to include those craftsmen who needed to be able to write for their craft, such as those who decorated the royal tomb. In the Nineteenth and Twentieth Dynasties, these people lived in a village on the desert edge at Thebes, close to their workplace in the Valley of the Kings. The dry ground of that village, now known as Deir el-Medina, preserved papyri well and the terrain was rich in pale limestone chippings, ideal for the supply of ostraca. Ironically, these sources reveal far more about the villagers than about the officials who once commanded them; most Egyptians did not record their lives on papyrus or any other medium.

The ability to write guaranteed some status in both this life and the next. Literary texts extolled the benefits of the career of a scribe and funerary texts secured eternal bliss for the deceased by giving him the position of secretary to a deity. Such was the prestige of writing that papyrus rolls were sometimes placed in the tomb, regardless of their texts, simply as a sign that the deceased belonged to the elite. To possess a papyrus written with a protective spell was as beneficial as knowing or reciting the spell, and amulets made out of papyri have been found (for example, BM EA 10731).

Hieroglyphs were termed the 'Words of God', perhaps from their close connection with divine images. Writing, wisdom, virtue and power were closely allied. In the Middle Kingdom *Tale of the Eloquent Peasant,* an official is addressed as the embodiment of these qualities in a scribal metaphor, 'O you reed, roll, palette of Thoth!'. Thoth was the god of knowledge and was connected with the moon, which was a means of calculating time. He was represented as a baboon and images of him in this form are shown watching over scribes as they write; statues of him were worshipped in record offices. Thoth's principal form, however, was as an ibis or as an ibis-headed god; in later times it was said that this was because the ibis searched in the ground as if it were looking for truth and knowledge. Although Thoth was often called the 'lord of the Words of God', writing itself was deified as the goddess Seshat, or less often as Nebetseshau, 'Lady of Writing'.

41

VII

The Egyptians considered writing to embody the essence of their civilisation, and monumental and literary texts were intended to 'speak to the future' and to be worthy of eternity. The power of writing can be seen in the practice of erasing the names of state enemies from all documents and inscriptions, thus condemning them to destruction. One Ramesside didactic text (BM EA 10684) extols literature as a cultural memorial: 'The roll is more excellent than the carved stela'. Another (BM EA 9994) extols the joys of writing:

Spend the day writing with your fingers
and read in the night!
Be close to the roll and the palette –
they are sweeter than pomegranate-wine.
Writing, for him who knows it,
is more excellent than any office.
It is sweeter than provisions and beer,
than clothing, than ointment.
It is more precious than a heritage in Egypt,
than a chapel in the West.

TYPES OF WRITINGS

The emergence of writing in Egypt, as in Mesopotamia and perhaps the Indus Valley, was closely associated with state administration, although religious activity may have provided an equal impulse. Egyptian hiero-glyphs obeyed the same rules of representation as formal art, of which they were an integral part. On monuments, writing first appeared as captions, to specify the subject represented or to provide the name of the owner: the bare name and list remained fundamental types of text. It was only in the Third and Fourth Dynasties that continuous texts began to be written. Throughout history the amount and range of writing expanded, although the early tradition of monumental display continued: the latest dated hieroglyphs are in a secondary inscription on a temple wall at

Philae in AD 394.

In the following pages, the different categories of texts are briefly described. From the Old Kingdom, there are the remains of various types of administrative documents, including decrees, letters and contracts. Official archives, discovered during the 1890s and 1970s in the Fifth Dynasty pyramid field of Abusir, cover a wide spectrum of work records, including even a pass to allow access to a restricted area of the pyramid complex. The monumental record of the end of this period also included a large body of royal funerary spells and rituals that were inscribed in the chambers of the royal pyramids (now known as the Pyramid Texts); linguistic evidence suggests that some of them were composed earlier, implying that they must have been passed down until then on papyrus or in oral form. Many of the texts, including decrees, eulogies, hymns and liturgies, had probably been transferred from papyri. Fragments of administrative texts survive from most periods and range from state archives to the business papers of individual officials. Legal documents are preserved from all the principal periods.

It is difficult to assess how much has been lost. The majority of administrative papyri will have been kept in the exposed environment of towns in the Nile valley and have decayed; funerary texts which were deposited in the dry sands of the cemeteries have fared better. There was presumably a vast mass of administrative paperwork, from which only a few examples have survived. Such practical documents and archives probably consumed the greatest quantities of papyrus: in the Graeco-Roman Period, an office of the minister Apollonios is known to have used an average of thirteen rolls a day for the period of 258–257 BC. One surviving roll of the state bureaucracy is a Ramesside account of crops in a part of Middle Egypt (now known as Papyrus Wilbour in the Brooklyn Museum, New York). The papyrus is 10.33 m long, with some four and a half thousand lines over one hundred and two pages, giving some impression of the amount of paperwork that was a feature of all periods. An earlier example is the fragmentary 'Semna despatches' (BM EA 10752, 10771), which comprises copies of reports from the fortresses in Nubia such as Semna; the reports indicate a similar obsession with detail in Middle Kingdom bureaucracy.

The Twelfth Dynasty seems to have witnessed a proliferation in the use of writing, although it is sometimes uncertain whether a genre that first appears then was an innovation or one that had existed earlier on manuscripts that have not survived. Religious texts on papyri included hymns and rituals and there were papyrus versions (BM EA 10676) of the Coffin Texts, the Middle Kingdom funerary texts that were written in cursive hieroglyphs on coffins of wealthy private individuals.

The Egyptian concept of literature was different to the modern one and can be defined as a body of written high culture which excluded the recording of practical information, such as administrative accounts. Literature consisted not only of fictional or poetic works but also of

B/w 177422

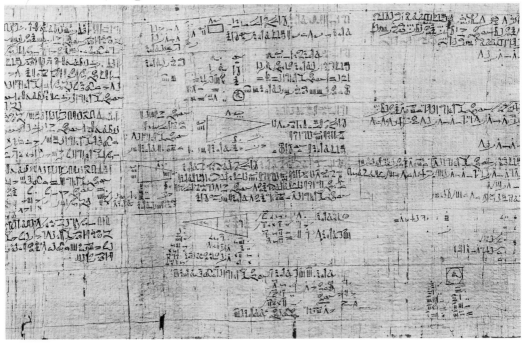

technical texts about mathematics and healing. These were not analytical discourses, but lists of problems and practices with encyclopaedic tendencies. The oldest surviving example is a papyrus of the early Middle Kingdom (now in the Egyptian Museum, Turin) with spells for healing, in this case against snakes and eye-ailments. It is clear from references in inscriptions that 'medical' texts had already existed in the Old Kingdom, although none are extant. Three early Eighteenth Dynasty papyri, which were probably found together in a tomb, are good examples of these technical texts. Firstly, Papyrus Ebers is a large compendium of prescriptions and contains signs added in the margin to note that a prescription had been 'used' or had been found 'good'. Secondly, in the Edwin Smith Surgical Papyrus (now in the New York Historical Society), injuries to the body are examined from the skull down, with diagnosis, prognosis and (if possible) a treatment. The third manual is the Rhind Mathematical Papyrus, which is a series of division tables and problems with solutions, intended to act as general models. Other similar texts list 'magical' spells, gynaecological and veterinary problems and other such examples. The Egyptian tradition of knowledge as compendia is epitomised in the so-called *Onomastica*, 'lists of words'. They simply list words in categories, although fragments show that such lists were sometimes expanded into treatises on, for example, types of serpents. One papyrus shows that a list could codify historical information: the fragmentary 'Turin Canon' lists the kings of Egypt and the length of each reign.

Also in the Twelfth Dynasty appeared imaginative 'literature' (in the narrow modern sense of the word). This had presumably existed earlier

34 *A section of the Rhind Mathematical Papyrus with problems concerning the calculation of area and volume, including illustrations. Second Intermediate Period, c.1550 BC, from Thebes. H. 32. cm. EA 10057, detail.*

34

in oral form, both in the formal setting of the royal court and at the level of folktales. The three main genres were didactic *Teachings*; reflective, often pessimistic, *Discourses*; and *Tales* which, like many other genres, were composed in verse. The acclaimed 'masterpiece' of Egyptian writing, the *Tale of Sinuhe*, illustrates the poetic mastery of these ancient authors. 9

In the New Kingdom both writing and types of written text proliferated. The late Eighteenth Dynasty saw the official written language of papyri change from Middle Egyptian (which was by then archaic), to the more 'colloquial' Late Egyptian. The Middle Kingdom literary works continued to be copied, but Late Egyptian tales began to be written in a style more similar to 'folktales' than that of earlier tales; these included the semi-mythical *Tale of the Two Brothers* (BM EA 10183). Teachings were also composed in Late Egyptian and new genres appeared, including scholastic *Miscellanies*. These were anthologies of short texts intended, in part, for teaching; manuscripts include didactic passages, model letters, lyrical panegyrics, hymns and prayers. In general, written literature broadened to include genres previously unrecorded on papyri, such as love songs. Texts from public contexts, such as commemorative inscriptions, were sometimes copied onto papyri and writing boards.

The funerary literary tradition continued to be written in formal Middle Egyptian but a major revision produced a new corpus first attested from the Seventeenth Dynasty on the coffin of Queen Mentuhotep (now unlocated and known only from hand copies of the hieratic texts by John Gardner Wilkinson, who presented them to the British Museum in 1834). From the reign of Hatshepsut, the revised corpus was copied onto papyri that were placed in wealthy burials (the *Books of the Dead*). At about the same date, the *Underworld Books*, which illustrate the p. 6 journey of the night sun, appeared on royal tomb walls in cursive hieroglyphs, as if imitating a papyrus. This and other features suggest that papyrus copies already existed by this date, and the works may have been composed as early as the Middle Kingdom. It is probable that in royal tombs painted walls and gilt wooden shrines were used for funerary texts, rather than papyri. Only one papyrus survives from an Eighteenth Dynasty royal tomb (that of Amenhotep II), but this may date to the Twenty-first Dynasty when the royal mummies were reburied. There was a papyrus charm around the neck of the mummy of Tutankhamen, but this disintegrated upon discovery.

Most genres are known by the New Kingdom. Traditions continued to be elaborated then and later, although the increasing variety of scripts may have restricted literacy more. Surviving papyri of the Third Intermediate Period are more limited in scope than those of the New Kingdom, probably because of the accidents of preservation. The centre of economic and political activity was by that time in the Delta, which is too humid to preserve organic matter such as papyrus. Almost all extant manuscripts from the Delta have survived only because they were acci- 54 dentally charred in fires. Most other surviving papyri from this period are funerary texts from Thebes, written in either cursive hieroglyphs or hieratic. In addition to *Book of the Dead* papyri, wealthy Theban burials normally included a second papyrus called the 'What is in the Underworld' (*Amduat*), which contained elements from the New Kingdom royal *Underworld Books*.

Few administrative documents or letters survive from the Third Intermediate Period, a position which changes with the introduction of demotic in the seventh century BC. A great number of demotic papyri are legal contracts ranging from sales of land to marriage contracts, providing a mass of detailed information. From the fourth century BC new literary texts in demotic are found, which continue the earlier traditions of tales and wisdom texts. Wisdom texts include the maxims of Papyrus Insinger (now in the Rijksmuseum, Leiden) and the more prosaic *Sayings of Ankhsheshonqy* replete with 'common sense' (BM EA 10508). The tales narrate deeds from the past, including the exploits of the family of the High Priest Khaemwaset, the son of Ramses II (for example, BM EA 10822), and the six tales of the *Cycle of Inaros and Petubastis* (for example, BM EA 10850), in which heroes vie for supremacy in epic style. Some of these perhaps show some influence from Greek epic. Alongside demotic, hieratic occasionally survived as a script for literature; there are hieratic manuscripts which contain a wisdom text (in the Brooklyn Museum, New York) and a tale (Papyrus Vandier, now in the university at Lille).

In the Late Period some ancient texts written in Old and Middle Egyptian were provided with translations into the contemporary vernacular; this had become necessary because the later phases of the language were as different from the classic Middle Egyptian phases as, for example, Italian is from Latin. After the conquest of the Persian Empire by Alexander the Great, texts continued to be composed in the native language and in the Ptolemaic Period, texts on temple walls collected or elaborated Pharaonic religious traditions. A surviving parallel on papyrus is a hieroglyphic manuscript concerning the sixteenth to eighteenth provinces of Upper Egypt, which is now known as Papyrus Jumilhac (now in the Louvre, Paris).

46   From the period of Roman rule the quantity of extant manuscripts in native scripts decreased. Demotic contracts became scarce and funerary papyri no longer contained a substantial *Book of the Dead* but short compositions such as the *Documents for Breathing*. Roman Egypt produced lengthy literary manuscripts in Egyptian as well as in Greek; one cycle of fables known today as the *Myth of the Eye of the Sun* existed in both Greek and Egyptian demotic versions. From the same period come copies of the *Book of the Fayum*, a diagram of the Fayum area accompanied by hieroglyphic texts reminiscent of the concerns of Papyrus Jumilhac. The only astronomical papyri from Egypt date from the late Ptolemaic and Roman Periods and are written in demotic; two provide a commentary on the astronomical ceiling in the cenotaph of Sety I at Abydos (then 1500 years old). It is possible that these types of text existed in earlier periods.

35 *Copy of an illustrated papyrus roll (Papyrus Ramesseum B) of a kingship ritual. The figures are drawn in a schematic style, similar to the cursive hieroglyphs of the text. The columns of text contain directions for the ritual, and are aligned to the relevant figures. Late Middle Kingdom, c.1800 BC, from Thebes. EA 10610, detail.*

36 *Part of the papyrus roll containing the* Book of the Dead *of the copyist Nebseny, in retrograde cursive hieroglyphs. The vignettes are drawn in black with occasional details in red. Here he and his wife receive offerings from their son (note the scribe's 'writing container' under the chair). Eighteenth Dynasty, c.1400 BC, from Saqqara. H. 33.5 cm. EA 9900.32, detail.*

ILLUSTRATIONS

The administrative papyri of the Old Kingdom included inventories in which objects were identified by name and by a larger version of the last sign in the word, the pictorial 'determinative'. These signs are virtually 'illustrations' to the 'text', but the earliest surviving papyrus with texts and separate vignettes dates to the Middle Kingdom. This is a ritual involving the statue of Senusret I at Karnak (Papyrus Ramesseum B, now BM EA 10610); this has stick-men, shaped like the cursive hieroglyphs in which the text was written. Other evidence suggests that papyri with a mixture of texts and pictures already existed in the Old Kingdom, although no examples survive.   35

The paintings on Middle Kingdom coffins imply that illustrations may have been painted on papyri, rather than being drawn in black ink. No such vignettes survive, apart from a couple of coloured fragments from Lahun. The New Kingdom *Book of the Dead* papyri were usually provided with vignettes for each spell, including a map of the 'Fields of Paradise' which was adapted from one in the earlier Coffin Texts. The vignettes were important parts of the book in themselves and not just illustrations accompanying the text. The best known is perhaps the scene complementing spell 125 in the *Book of the Dead* in which the heart of the deceased   VII
is weighed against Truth. The vignettes were coloured and the styles of different periods range from drawings in black and red to a fully painterly approach (such as the sumptuous Papyrus of Ani, BM EA 10470). Gilding   V–VII
was rare; one *Book of the Dead* with gilt decoration belonged, significantly, to a master goldsmith. On one New Kingdom manuscript (BM EA 9900)   36

the illustrations were completely uncoloured; this belonged to a temple copyist named Nebseny, who may have drawn his own vignettes rather than use an illustrator.

After the New Kingdom, *Book of the Dead* papyri contain more uncoloured vignettes, such as the finely drawn vignettes of Nestanebtisheru (BM EA 10554), where the rough under-sketch in red is still clearly visible. The illustrations were sometimes painted before the text was written and the painter did not always leave enough space for the text. Illustrations could also be painted in later, sometimes being done in the wrong order, or even not at all: a papyrus in the Metropolitan Museum of Art, New York, has a blank space with a note to the illustrator: 'To be done like the images in the (original) writings'.

p. 6   In the New Kingdom *Underworld Books* the pictorial matter was an integral part of the whole, as much as the cursive hieroglyphic text. These compositions were often elaborately executed. In later papyrus versions of the earliest composition, the *Amduat*, the colours are usually the scribe's basic black and red, and the illustrations are schematic, with stick figures. In the late Twenty-first Dynasty, papyri appear composed almost exclusively of vignettes from a variety of earlier funerary compositions.

     The later Eighteenth Dynasty provides a tantalising glimpse of the wide range of illustrated papyri that once existed outside the funerary sphere. A few fragments from a chapel in the Residence city of Akhenaten at Amarna contain a battle scene in which Egyptian troops are fighting against enemies of western nomadic stock (BM EA 74100). This type of scene is otherwise completely unknown on papyri.

37   The late New Kingdom has left other sparse traces of a wider secular tradition of art. These include some satirical papyri, possibly from Deir el-Medina, which show animals acting out human roles (for example BM EA 10016); one also has a series of ribald vignettes of sexual intercourse, a subject excluded from formal art (now in the Egyptian Museum, Turin).

37   *Fragments of a painted roll from a shrine at Amarna. This is a unique example of a battle scene on papyrus. The reassembled pieces show Egyptian troops, and an Egyptian being killed by Libyan archers. Late Eighteenth Dynasty, c.1350 BC, from Amarna. H. of main fragment 6.3 cm. EA 74100, detail.*

38

38 *Part of the 'Satirical Papyrus', a roll containing a series of coloured illustrations in which animals are given human roles. Nineteenth or Twentieth Dynasty, c.1200 BC, from Thebes. H. 9 cm. EA 10016, detail.*

39 *Copy of a papyrus bearing a plan of the tomb of Ramses IV in the Valley of the Kings, with measurements and names of chambers in hieratic. Original in the Egyptian Museum, Turin; late Twentieth Dynasty, c.1100 BC, from Thebes. H. 24.5 cm. Drawing by Richard Lepsius (1867).*

Another papyrus in Turin preserves the only surviving map: a schematic diagram showing the route to the gold mines along the Wadi Hammamat. Plans were also drawn on papyri, as is shown by a coloured plan for the tomb of Ramses IV in the Valley of the Kings. A Ramesside papyrus with two elevations of a wooden shrine looks like a working diagram and a Ptolemaic papyrus has two elevations of a statue of a sphinx, with a grid to help transfer the design onto a block of stone (now in the Egyptian Museum, Berlin). Another example contains a design of a hieroglyphic inscription for a door. Pattern books probably existed for projects such as monumental reliefs and paintings.

39

STORING PAPYRI: LIBRARIES AND ARCHIVES

Rolls would on the whole be stored with the recto inside, although a few have been discovered with the recto outside, as if they had not been rerolled after someone had read the text on the verso. The hieroglyphic sign for a book shows a rolled papyrus with ties and a seal: Texts often included titles, or a précis at the start, which could be read by unrolling the first page of the papyrus. Legal documents seem sometimes to have had a short title on the verso which was visible when the document was rolled (for example, BM EA 10612); this was presumably for easy access in a legal archive. Such titles written along the outside of a roll have rarely been noticed on other types of text, although some are known

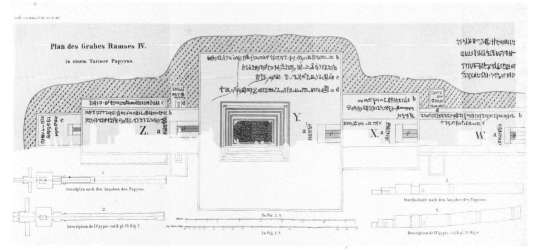

from New Kingdom and Third Intermediate Period funerary papyri. One earlier *Book of the Dead* (Eighteenth Dynasty, BM EA 10489) has a single horizontal line written along the verso containing an offering formula, but this is not a title and none of it was visible when the papyrus was rolled. The details of a roll's contents may have been written, when necessary, on the container in which it was stored. Some funerary papyri of the Third Intermediate Period have the word 'top' written on the outside of the top of the roll, but this was presumably so that they were placed in the tomb the right way up, not to prevent a reader from unrolling them upside down.

Rolls have been found in jars; sometimes these jars had been buried in tombs, but they were also used for storage in daily life. One Ptolemaic demotic archive of over thirty documents was found in two jars in the remains of a house on the west bank at Thebes. Although jars were widely used in earlier periods, the preferred method of storage was probably to place the rolls in a chest; this is how the 'Ramesseum papyri' (see p. 62) were found and is also how literary tales describe stored rolls. A copy of a cycle of love songs from Deir el-Medina states that the original was 'found in a book-container', and a Ramesside representation of a records office shows rows of chests. Surviving chests for other types of object sometimes have hieratic notes on the outside listing their contents; a few faience plaques exist that seem to have been attached to or inlaid in chests storing royal manuscripts. One from Thebes has the names of Amenhotep III and Queen Tiy and the title 'The Book of the Moringa Tree', suggesting that the box may have held a single roll. There is an earlier example with the cartouches of Amenemhat IV. In tombs funerary texts were often placed directly on or inside the coffin, but in the Ramesside Period and the Third Intermediate Period some funerary papyri were stored inside hollow figures of the god Ptah-Sokar-Osiris; the papyri of Hunefer and Anhay were found in such figures (BM EA 9901 in 9861 and BM EA 10472 in 20868).

A royal investigation of state archives is described in the stela erected by King Neferhotep of the Thirteenth Dynasty to commemorate his refurbishment of the Temple of Osiris at Abydos. To guide his restoration, the king declares his desire to:

> *see the writings of Primeval times of Atum,*
> *Open (them) for me, for an inventory!*

He is answered by the courtiers:

> *'May your Majesty proceed to the Houses of Writings and see the Words of God (i.e. the hieroglyphs)!'*
> *His Majesty proceeded to the House of the Book.*
> *And then his Majesty opened the writings with these Courtiers.*
> *Then his Majesty found the writings of the Temple of Osiris Foremost of Westerners.*

40 *Two plaques, perhaps originally tied to or inserted into the side of containers. One bears the names of Amenemhat IV; the other names Amenhotep III, and a line at the base gives the title 'The Book of the Moringa Tree'. Blue glazed composition; Twelfth Dynasty, c.1800 BC, H. 6.3 cm, EA 22879; Eighteenth Dynasty, c.1350 BC, H. 5.5 cm, EA 22878.*

The reverence paid to ancient writings, which is attested in many Egyptian texts, implies that there was a concern for long term storage. The 'House of the Book' that King Neferhotep visits was a temple library. As well as these religious archives, there were working administrative archives in which the principle of storage with a view to easy retrieval seems to have been effectively implemented. At Memphis, the tomb-chapel inscription of a Ramesside official, Mose, records a lawsuit over land, during which documents had to be checked in the relevant state offices, some dating from over two centuries earlier. Administrative archives included official daybooks listing the daily economic activity of an institution; into such a roll official letters could be copied rather than being archived, as was explicitly requested in one letter sent to the Middle Kingdom temple at Lahun.

The papyri from the town at Lahun might have provided an opportunity to study the original context of such working archives but few records were kept of where they were found on the site in 1889. Fragments of a business archive survive from the temple area and the town site produced several groups of papyri. One excavated lot contains a literary tale, written on the verso of a set of hymns to Senusret III, a veterinary papyrus, mathematical texts and accounts of people associated with the priestly sphere. This was presumably an archive connected with the temple. Another temple archive consisted entirely of business letters and accounts.

The importance of libraries is clear from surviving manuscripts. For example, New Kingdom *Book of the Dead* papyri were compiled from master copies in libraries and some manuscripts provide very garbled texts. One of the best extant texts is the papyrus of Nebseny, who was a 'Copyist in the Temples of the North and South' at Memphis, and as such evidently had access to the master copies of the temple libraries (BM EA 9900). Another Eighteenth Dynasty man, Nebimes, was less scrupulous; he appropriated a leather master copy of the *Book of the Dead* by squeezing his name into the space where it had 'such-and-such a person' (BM EA 10281).

The only preserved Pharaonic record office is that in the unique site of Amarna. The central area of the city included a building complex designated the 'Place of Documents of Pharaoh'. One of these buildings housed a working archive not of papyri but of hundreds of tablets inscribed with texts in the cuneiform script of Western Asia. These were mostly diplomatic correspondence, but there were examples of other genres, including myths, epics and lexical lists. On the sides of some tablets short record notes had been written in hieratic; this implies that there was an Egyptian filing system for the tablets. They may have been arranged on shelves as in Mesopotamia, but the building was too badly damaged to be certain.

The Theban tomb of Tjay, a royal scribe under Merenptah, includes an image of a 'Place of the Documents of Pharaoh'. The entrance is shown leading into a courtyard flanked by two porticoes, under which sit scribes writing at their chests. Another door leads into a pillared hall in which Tjay is making an offering on an altar; at the end of this room is a raised area from which three doors open. The central one, flanked by two statues of baboons, leads into a chapel to the baboon god Thoth; the two rooms either side of the chapel are captioned 'the places of writings' and their walls are lined with a row of chests presumably containing manuscripts.

In the same area of Amarna as the 'Place of Documents' was a building complex which was identified by stamps on its bricks as a 'House of Life'; in this a few fragments of painted papyrus were found (now in the Ashmolean Museum, Oxford). Graeco-Roman texts present the House of Life as the workplace of the sacred scribes and it seems to have been an institution in which scholarly and sacred texts were copied and compiled – a more active version of the House of the Books in which the texts were stored for reference. As the home to the core of the educated Egyptian elite, the House of Life functioned as the kernel of their culture, which came to an end when the temples ceased to maintain this institution.

The only temple library building to have survived intact is in the Ptolemaic temple of Edfu. It is a small low room built between two columns of the screen wall between the open court and the great columned hall; like the symmetrically placed vestry it was entered from

this hall. It was named the 'House of the Book' and the wall inscriptions include a list of book-titles, some of which match rituals attested on papyri from burials of the fourth to third centuries BC. In the walls are two small niches, which presumably contained caskets with rolls. The contents will not have been the full temple library, but only the ritual texts and liturgies that were used in the current ceremonies. The full temple library would have embraced a wider range of written culture, as is seen in the Roman Period priestly libraries of Tebtunis in the Fayum, whose manuscripts survive in thousands of fragments. These are enough to show that the libraries included such texts as a copy of Middle Kingdom funerary inscriptions from Asyut, then two thousand years old. These unique fragments indicate how rich the contents of these lost collections may have been.

Private Archives

An early example of a small working family archive consists of Middle Kingdom legal papyri from Lahun. One document records the cession of Asiatic servants from one brother to another; in a second document, written a generation later, the same servants were bequeathed with other property to the brother's wife. Personal collections of legal and other documents are more common from the Late Period, when substantial batches of contracts were buried with individuals. Late Period and Ptolemaic demotic family archives survive from numerous different parts of the country, rather than being restricted, like papyri of earlier periods, to a handful of specific locations, clustering in the areas of Thebes and Memphis.

Other groups of papyri seem, however, to be bundles of discarded post rather than longer term archives. These include the lively Heqanakht letters of the early Middle Kingdom. One collection of late Ramesside letters spanning more than a decade seems to have been a family archive.

These are the correspondence of the royal craftsman Butehamen and his father Thutmes (nicknamed Tjaroy), from the very end of the New Kingdom. The letters provide remarkable glimpses of personal opinion, most strikingly in one from the king's general to Tjaroy, in which he remarks with undisguised contempt 'whose master is Pharaoh these days?'.

Two surviving individual libraries of papyri show that the scope of personal collections could go far beyond practical everyday papers. The first of these is from the Thirteenth Dynasty and is known as the Ramesseum library since it was found in a plundered tomb under the precinct of the later Ramesseum. The name of the tomb-owner is unknown but he is generally considered to have been a priest. The shaft contained a chest with a jackal on the lid, which was perhaps a funerary symbol or connected with the priestly title 'Master of Secrets' (written with a hieroglyph of a jackal). In the chest, which is now unlocated, was a group of magical equipment and a collection of over twenty rolls. The contents of these included four literary texts, an onomasticon, a series of hymns to Sobek, two rituals, and various medical and magical texts (BM EA 10610, 10752–72, with two in the Egyptian Museum, Berlin).

The other library came from Deir el-Medina. Many of the manuscripts are now known as Papyrus Chester Beatty after their first modern owner, Sir Alfred Chester Beatty (1875–1968). They were scattered after their discovery; most are in the British Museum (BM EA 10682–99), but one is in the Chester Beatty Library and Gallery in Dublin and others are in the Institut Français d'Archéologie Orientale in Cairo, and the Ashmolean Museum in Oxford. The collection includes a wide variety of texts: there is the family archive of letters, memoranda and inheritance documents, texts dealing with private affairs of a related family and official matters and (as in the Ramesseum Papyri), literary texts, hymns and texts of healing. These last were often copied on the same roll; thus one roll (BM EA 10685) contains the *Hymn to the Inundation*, a literary *Miscellany*, and texts of healing. The principal ritual text in the collection is for the daily cult of Amen and the dead king Amenhotep I (BM EA 10689). The technical texts include the only surviving book about the interpretation of dreams (the so-called *Dream Book*, BM EA 10683). Literary works include the *Scribal Controversy* (BM EA 10697), the Middle Kingdom *Teaching of Khety* and the Late Egyptian *Teaching of Any* (BM EA 10699, *Miscellanies* (BM EA 10684 verso), the *Tale of Truth and Falsehood* (BM EA 10682), the *Tale of Horus and Seth* (Papyrus Chester Beatty 1 in Dublin), and cycles of love poems (on the verso of the last).

This collection of over forty papyri was built up over more than a century by successive owners until it was deposited in a tomb-chapel; the history of its owners has been reconstructed in some detail by P. W. Pestman. The first was an imperious but learned scribe with antiquarian interests, Qenherkhopshef, who was born in year 16 of Ramses II (*c*.1274 BC) and who died under Saptah aged about 70. He collected literary

12, 35, 53

43

42

42 *Part of a papyrus roll with the* Dream Book *written in a fine literary hand on the recto (top). On the verso (bottom) is a copy of the* Battle of Qadesh *written by the craftsman Qenherkhepshef. On the recto, a later owner, Amennakht, has added his own colophon. Note the fine narrow sheet-joins. Nineteenth and Twentieth Dynasties, from Thebes, c.1275 to 1175 BC.* H. *34.5 cm.* EA *10683,2.*

manuscripts, including the *Dream Book* onto which he himself copied the
epic poem of the *Battle of Qadesh* in his unmistakable hand (BM EA 10683).
A papyrus charm worn by him survives (BM EA 10731). At his death the
papyri went to his second wife Niutnakht, whose will was later included in
the archive (now in the Ashmolean Museum, Oxford). The will does not
mention the papyri, but from the letters, memoranda and colophons in
the group it seems that she left them to her second husband Khaemnun,
from whom they passed to a son of Khaemnun and Niutnakht, Amennakht. Although he was a simple workman, he was literate – and proud of
it. He took great care of the library, copying his name onto his stepfather's

42

B/w 270837.

Dream Book. He added to the library the magnificent copy of the *Tale of Horus and Seth*, which was given to him by his close friend Nakhtsobek. The fifth owner was Amennakht's brother, Maanakhtef, a carpenter. The archive includes one of his letters on an apparently fresh sheet, but he cut up some literary rolls to provide sheets for his business correspondence and even the *Dream Book* was torn after generations of preservation.

The later scribe Tjaroy, well known from the late Ramesside letters, answers in one letter an enquiry from his son Butehamen about a library – 'the matter of the writings which are deposited in the chapel of the tomb-shaft'. This library may have been the same collection as Qenherkhopshef's, some of which was then almost two centuries old. Tjaroy wrote,

Now as for the writings on which the sky rained in the house of the scribe Horsheri my <forefather>, you brought them outside and we found that they had not been erased. I said to you 'I will unbind them again (to dry them out)'. You brought them below, and we deposited them in the tomb-chapel of Amennakht my forefather. (BM EA 10326)

43 One roll of the Chester Beatty library, the *Ritual of Amenhotep I*, still bears traces of dirt, as if from having been unrolled damp on the ground by Tjaroy. And it is possible that they remained in the same tomb-chapel (no. 1165) in the cemetery at Deir el-Medina until 1928 when the excavator Bernard Bruyère's workmen found them there.

43 *End of a papyrus roll containing the* Ritual of Amenhotep I. *The first phrase of the colophon is written in red. The surface of this roll bears traces of mud, thickest in the grooves between fibres. Nineteenth Dynasty, c.1225 BC, from Thebes. EA 10689.8, detail.*

CHAPTER FOUR

Usage and Survival outside Pharaonic Egypt

Papyri! Insects gnaw them. Time corrodes
and native plants get potted in a mulch of Pindar's Odes!
Horrible to contemplate! How can a person sleep
while Sophocles is rotting on an ancient rubbish heap?
T. Harrison, The Trackers of Oxyrhynchus

P apyrus was not used just by the Egyptians but by most societies of the ancient Mediterranean world. Few papyri, however, have survived the usually unsuitable climatic conditions outside the dry areas of Upper Egypt and the Fayum. Papyri from elsewhere have been discovered mainly in the Near East, but a few are known from Greece and Italy. The oldest preserved papyrus from outside Egypt was written in Hebrew (*c.*750 BC) and comes from Murabba'at, a cave by the Dead Sea. Some of the later Dead Sea Scrolls were written on papyrus. In Egypt the large number of papyri which survive from all periods allow the material to be studied at first hand. As already mentioned, many of these papyri are written in Greek, since this became the main administrative language after the conquest of Egypt by Alexander the Great in 332 BC. In general, they are less well preserved than Pharaonic papyri, having come mainly from rubbish heaps rather than cemeteries.

CLASSICAL PAPYRI

When the ancient Greeks thought of a book they had a papyrus roll in mind. The earliest Greek papyrus fragments come from Greece and all are grave goods. Until 1982, the papyrus from Derveni in Macedonia, dated to the fourth century BC, was the earliest known. It contains a commentary on Orphic verses. In 1982, however, burnt fragments of a papyrus were found in a tomb at Athens, along with other

44

EASTERN MEDITERRANEAN

Ravenna
Rimini
ITALY
Rome
Herculaneum
Pompeii
Palermo
SICILY
Syracuse

MACEDONIA
GREECE
Athens

BLACK SEA

Byzantium (Istanbul)

ANATOLIA

Pergamon

CRETE
MEDITERRANEAN SEA

CYPRUS

SYRIA
PHOENICIA
Byblos

Megiddo
PALESTINE
River Jordan

Alexandria

SINAI

0   500 kms
0   300 mls

EGYPT

Nile

goods that could be dated to the fifth century BC. This papyrus is badly preserved and is not yet published, but it is probably the earliest extant Greek papyrus.

44 *Map of the eastern Mediterranean.*

45   Classical authors provide some evidence that the use of papyrus rolls in Greece must have been established by the sixth century BC. The main sources, however, are the surviving examples from Egypt, which give an idea of the original appearance and form of texts that were otherwise only preserved in much later medieval manuscripts. From these it is clear that Greek was written on papyri with the sheet-joins left over right to accommodate the direction of the script. The text was written in pages of

46   columns, whose widths vary with the type of text and the handwriting. A single papyrus roll could contain more than one work, and at the end of such rolls the titles of the works would be listed; sometimes when a roll contained only one work the title was written on a tag attached to it. Papyri may have been rolled around a rod, unlike in the Pharaonic Period.

The most famous library in classical antiquity was that of Alexandria, the centre of the Hellenistic intellectual world. It was founded probably by Ptolemy I and extended by Ptolemy II and it may have contained more than half a million volumes. Its librarians, some of whom were also famous as poets, collected texts and pioneered editing practices which remain the basis of present textual scholarship. The texts were mostly classical, and it is not known if the library contained any Egyptian writings. The library continued to exist, even after the famous fire during the siege of Alexandria by Julius Caesar, until the seventh century, when the city was sacked by the Arabs.

In many cases handwriting is the only means of dating papyri, particularly literary copies. These are often written in a 'book hand' which was carefully executed with concern for an attractive appearance. In such a hand each individual letter was written separately, without any ligatures. Literary texts were also sometimes annotated, with comments in the margin referring to difficult passages and explaining unusual words. To judge from surviving papyri, the most copied work was Homer's *Iliad*, which some readers may have found difficult: it is the oldest surviving piece of Greek literature and is written in a dialect and style that would have been unfamiliar to a reader in Roman Egypt. At Hawara in 1889 the Egyptologist W. M. Flinders Petrie found the coffin of an unnamed young woman with a carefully written roll of the second book of the *Iliad* placed under her head. The second most popular author was the classical playwright Euripides.

As well as 'book hand', there was 'cursive' or 'documentary' script. This writing was joined up and used most commonly in non-literary papyri. Writing was probably almost always done by professional scribes and it is by no means clear how much of the Greek-speaking population of Egypt was able to read. Signatures on official documents can be very clumsy, and sometimes the person was unable to sign which meant that the scribe would sign on their behalf. Signatures were not a practice of Pharaonic Egypt.

The majority of surviving classical texts are documentary and include a wide variety of types, such as contracts for sales, accounts and private letters. Some entire archives are preserved, including the famous archive of a business man named Zenon from the Ptolemaic Period. For Ptolemaic and Roman Egypt these archives provide a vast amount of primary source material which is exceptional in ancient classical history. Papyri are still providing new insights into literature. Before the discovery of papyri, some Greek authors were known only by name, or with hardly anything of their works surviving. Previously, for example, the comedies of the fourth-century author Menander were unknown and their discovery transformed the appreciation of ancient comedy. The *Constitution of the Athenians*, probably written by a pupil of Aristotle, was unknown before a roll was acquired by the British Museum (now in the British Library). Other 'rediscovered' authors include Sappho and Bacchylides, but often the identity of the author cannot be told from the fragments. The tantalizingly small size of most of these fragments and the number of unattributed pieces are a useful reminder that modern knowledge of classical antiquity is based on a relatively small and partial selection of texts.

Latin texts are found in Egypt from the period after 31 BC, when Egypt became part of the Roman Empire. Literary manuscripts also provide copies of Latin works, such as a fragment of Vergil from Hawara and a fragment of the hitherto almost unattested poetry of Gallus from the Lower Nubian fortress site of Qasr Ibrim; this site has produced texts from the Graeco-Roman Period up to AD 1464. Nevertheless, Greek remained the principal language of the administration in Egypt, and throughout the eastern provinces.

COPTIC AND LATER PAPYRI

From the third century BC, Greek letters were occasionally used by writers of Egyptian and in the second century AD the Egyptians began to adopt the Greek script with six additional letters derived from demotic to write the Egyptian language. Versions of Biblical scriptures translated from Greek were in use at the end of the third century AD, and almost a quarter of the vocabulary is derived from Greek. The word 'Coptic' is used not only of the script and the language, but of the local Church and Christian Egypt in general. 'Coptic' is derived from the Arabic form of the Greek *Aiguptios*, 'Egyptian'.

Coptic papyri cover the full range of Christian writing in Egypt, from accounts and letters to sermons and Biblical literature. The bulk of Coptic literature in the fourth and fifth centuries consists of translations from the Greek Biblical texts and writings of early Church fathers. Later literature was also almost exclusively religious. The most important Coptic author was Shenute, the abbot of the White Monastery in Upper Egypt *c.*AD 385–466, whose writings reveal his influence in the Coptic Church, and were read for many generations. His prose is strikingly passionate and individual.

46 Part of a papyrus roll containing prescriptions and incantations written partly in demotic and partly in Greek. Below one page the scribe has drawn an udjat eye, symbol of wholeness. Both texts are written with a Greek-style pen. Roman Period, c. third century AD, provenance unknown. H. 19.5 cm. EA 10588, recto and verso.

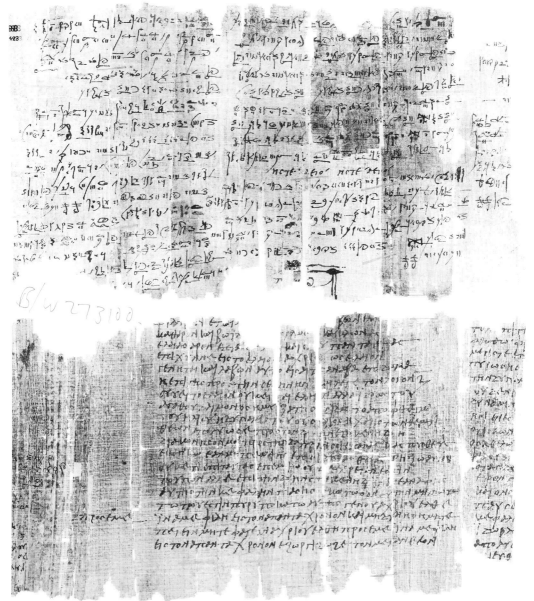

The most celebrated discovery of Coptic papyri was made in 1945 at Nag Hammadi when a cache was found by local inhabitants and dispersed on the market. It contained papyrus codices written in the fourth century, most of which contained Coptic translations of Greek texts and totalled over 1200 pages. There are fifty-one texts, thirty-six of which were previously unknown; these are a major source for the history of gnosticism and the early Church.

In the sixth to fourth centuries BC the Persian conquerors of Egypt had used Aramaic for their administration; major archives of Aramaic papyri have been discovered at Elephantine on the southern border. In AD

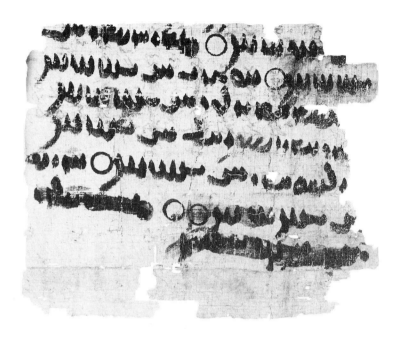

47 *Fragment of papyrus with Pahlavi script, probably dating to the brief Persian occupation of Egypt toward the end of Byzantine rule. Early seventh century AD, from the Fayum area. Courtesy of the Austrian National Library.*

619–629, Egypt was briefly occupied by the Sassanian Persian Empire and administrative papyri are found with another foreign script and language, Pahlavi. The Arab conquest of AD 641 put an end to Byzantine rule, although for the first fifty years the Arab government continued to use scribes who wrote in Greek before adopting Arabic for administration. Seventh-century documents were still written on papyrus, mixing Arabic and Greek, while Coptic remained in use in Church circles. During the following century Greek fell from use and Coptic dwindled under social forces and religious discrimination. As a spoken language of Upper Egypt it survived in places until the end of the sixteenth century and it is still used today in the services of the Coptic Church.

THE DEATH OF PAPYRUS

Although papyrus was very common as a writing surface in classical antiquity, there were alternatives (see also chapter 1). The Greeks as well as the Egyptians resorted to potsherds; in the Athenian assembly they used them to inscribe the names of the leaders whom they wanted to remove from office, hence the term 'ostracism' from ostraca. Where no papyrus plant was available, other plants were employed, as Pliny the Elder noted in his *Natural History*. In Germany, some coins appear to have been wrapped up in a piece of papyrus-like material that was actually made from willow which grew locally.

Leather and parchment were also much used and these eventually superseded papyrus. Parchment is specially treated leather, which is very supple and durable, especially in moister northern climates. Pliny the Elder related an anecdote that the Ptolemaic rulers of Egypt became jealous of the growing library at Pergamon (in modern Turkey), a possible rival to their library at Alexandria: they then prevented supplies of papyrus from reaching Pergamon and this supposedly resulted in the development of parchment (the word for which derives from the name of that city). However, other classical sources state that people in Near Eastern areas generally preferred parchment to papyrus, which suggests that leather was established as a writing surface in the Mediterranean world, as it had been in Pharaonic Egypt.

The replacement of papyrus by parchment probably reflects not the respective qualities of the two as writing surfaces, but the fact that parchment can be manufactured anywhere, as its raw material is not as geographically restricted as the papyrus plant.

It was not only the writing material that changed: the actual shape of a book was transformed. The joined wax-coated writing tablet had long

48 *A page from a codex made of thick sheets of papyrus. The text is a life of the abbot Shenute, written in the Sahidic dialect of Coptic. Only some fragments of leather and string survive from the codex binding. Seventh century AD, provenance unknown. H. 20.2 cm. EA 71005.10.*

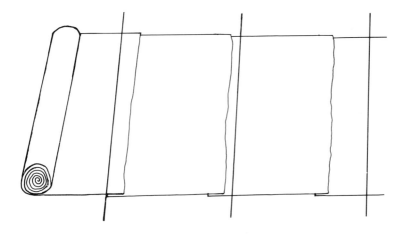

been known in Greece and had possibly come there from Phoenicia. In the Roman Period, small books of less than ten wooden pages began to be produced; some examples have recently been excavated in Dakhla Oasis in Egypt. A group of wooden tablets with Latin documents has survived even in Britain, at the fort of Vindolanda; these provide a remarkable glimpse of life on Hadrian's Wall.

48, 49   The papyrus roll was slowly replaced by the codex, which is similar in appearance to these wooden books. A codex is made of a group of papyrus or parchment sheets folded in the middle, producing a sort of pamphlet; this is essentially the model of the modern book. In the second half of the first century BC, the Roman poet Martial described such codices as being used for pocket editions of his poems, but the earliest extant examples date from the second to third centuries AD. Most early Christian texts, such as the Nag Hammadi library, survive on codices rather than rolls and this has led to a suggestion that the increasing popularity of the codex was connected with the rise of Christianity. This theory is, however, doubtful: the advantages of the codex over a long roll are obvious; it is easier to use for reference, to handle and to store. By the middle of the fourth century, the codex had become the accepted form of the book and Constantius II (AD 337–361) instructed the scribes of the Pergamon library to copy the texts that were preserved on papyrus rolls onto parchment codices. Some English medieval officials, however, reverted to scrolls.

Although papyrus was still occasionally used, such cases were probably exceptions rather than the rule. There is a Latin papyrus dated to 3 June AD 572; it concerns the sale of a farm and a house in the territory of Rimini and was written by Johannis Forensis of Ravenna. (This was the first papyrus acquired by the British Museum, in 1789, and is now in the British Library.) The latest certain dates for extant papyri are from 1057 (a papal decree) and 1087 (an Arabic document). Papyrus continued to be used in Byzantium until about AD 1100, but no examples have survived.

49 *How a codex was made up from a roll of papyrus. First, a roll was cut into sheets, and then the sheets were folded and gathered into a pamphlet.*

Both papyrus and parchment were eventually superseded by paper. Tradition ascribes the invention of paper to Cai Lun, a eunuch at the court of the Han emperor Wu Di (AD 105). It is said to have come westwards through prisoners of war taken by Arabs in the eighth century and within a century 'Samarkand paper' had replaced Egyptian papyrus as the writing material of the Arab Caliphate. It spread further west with the Arab conquests of Sicily and Spain. Paper was made from cloth, and at the end of the twelfth century, Abd al-Latif of Baghdad remarked that the mummy-wrappings of ancient Egyptians, for whom writing had meant papyrus, were being used to manufacture paper.

THE REDISCOVERY OF PAPYRI

Although European visitors to Egypt in the sixteenth and seventeenth centuries knew nothing of the Egyptian language, hieroglyphs inspired a lively interest and were considered a profound enigma. The first record of a cursive hieroglyphic document is in the *Voyages et Observations* of the French traveller Sieur de la Boullaye-le-Gouz (1657), who copied nine lines of cursive hieroglyphs 'found on the belt of a mummy'; this manuscript (now known to be part of a *Book of the Dead*) may have been a linen shroud rather than a roll of papyrus.

In the late eighteenth century travellers brought back individual pieces from Egypt, including a roll in Greek that was presented to the Italian prelate Stefano Borgia in 1778; the text was one of a large number then reported from the Fayum area and contains a long list of workmen on dykes near Tebtunis (now in Museo Nazionale in Naples). This sudden popularity of papyri was a result of the discovery of papyri in the ashes of the town of Herculaneum in Italy, an event that captured the imaginations of kings and scholars across Europe. In the 1750s, a large Roman villa was excavated and, among finds of magnificent sculptures, a library of over a thousand papyri was unearthed. After the eruption of Mount Vesuvius in AD 79, they had been preserved under the volcanic tufa; they were burnt and in a desperate condition, but still some attempts at conservation were carried out. The contents were not the lost works of famous poets, as was hoped, but a library of philosophical writings.

The collecting of Egyptian papyri began in earnest with the French occupation of Egypt under Napoleon Bonaparte in 1798–1801. According to the romantic account by Vivant Denon, the first papyri to be discovered by the French scholars were two rolls on a mummy at Thebes (these were bought in 1827 for the Tsar and are now in the Hermitage, St Petersburg). Such manuscripts remained unreadable until the decipherment first of demotic by Thomas Young in the 1810s and then of hieroglyphic by Jean François Champollion in 1822.

The large scale discovery of Greek and Latin papyri began in 1877 with Byzantine archives in the Fayum, but a dozen years passed before earlier classical manuscripts came to light. The discoveries of W. M. Flinders Petrie at Hawara in 1889 yielded ancient copies of authors

50 *A scene from Tony Harrison's play* The Trackers of Oxyrhynchus, *showing the recovery of papyrus fragments. Courtesy of the Royal National Theatre.*

previously known only from medieval manuscripts and in 1892 the Egyptologist Edouard Naville discovered an entire public archive at Mendes in the Delta, dating from the reign of Marcus Aurelius (AD 161–80), which had been burnt in a revolt.

The prospect of further discoveries attracted classical scholars such as Bernard Grenfell and Arthur Hunt to explore Oxyrhynchus in Middle Egypt and other sites in the Fayum. They excavated the town rubbish dumps and found huge numbers of scraps of papyrus, most of which are now in the Ashmolean Museum, Oxford. The first seasons produced verses of Sappho and part of a lost satyr play, the *Ichneutae*, by Sophocles (the only substantial surviving example of the genre). The discovery of 50   this play is in turn the subject of Tony Harrison's play, *The Trackers of Oxyrhynchus*, first performed at Delphi in 1988.

DAMAGE, SURVIVAL AND CONSERVATION

Although flexible when newly made, papyrus was always subject to tears and breaks at the hands of scribes and readers. Erasure and reuse inflict controlled damage to the surface, but careless handing means that it becomes abraded and the edges become worn. If kept in unsuitable conditions papyrus can suffer through hydrolysis, becoming more yellow-brown, or oxidation, becoming weaker and more brittle. A sheet can eventually decay into a skeleton of fibres and a handful of dust. When in storage, a roll can grow mould or rot with the damp and can be eaten by rodents or insects, particularly by white ants, when it is buried. These problems were present in antiquity, as is shown by examples of contem-

51   poraneous patching, and by the theological inscription on the 'Shabaka
52   Stone' (BM EA 498). This claims, in lines that reverse the message of the usual scribal colophon (see p. 29), that

52 *Detail of the Shabaka Stone. The upper line (right to left) gives the names and titles of the king, while the second (left to right) tells how he found the text on a roll 'eaten by worms' (note the serpent hieroglyph). Twenty-fifth Dynasty, c.700 BC, from Memphis. H. of lower band of text 2.2 cm. EA 498, detail.*

51 *A patch on the edge of the papyrus (lower centre) containing the* Book of the Dead *of Ani; since the roll was intended for burial, the damage and repair presumably happened during production. Nineteenth Dynasty, c.1250 BC, from Thebes. H. of the double band between vignette and blank margin 1.7 cm.* EA *10470.4, detail.*

*this writing was copied out anew by his Majesty
in the Temple of his father Ptah-south-of-his-wall,
for his Majesty had found it to be a work of the ancestors
which was worm eaten
and could not be understood from beginning to end.*

King Shabaka copied it onto a basalt slab 'so that it became better than it had been before'. Ironically, the slab was reused as a grindstone and is itself now illegible in many places.

The manner in which a papyrus was discovered in modern times has often compounded the damage. It was said in 1778 that papyri found at Giza were burnt by locals because of the pleasant smell of the smoke; according to another anecdote, when the chest containing the Ramesseum Papyri was being lifted out of the tomb-shaft, the rope broke and it fell into a puddle. Both of these are apocryphal, but it is true that many papyri were not excavated in ideal conditions.

The bulk of the work on papyri by the Department of Conservation in the British Museum is dealing with previously treated material acquired from travellers and collectors of the early nineteenth century. At that date complete papyri were unrolled directly onto backings of white or coloured paper or card. Once unrolled, the papyri were cut into con-

5, 14, 61, VIII

venient sections for mounting, with little regard for their content. They were then most commonly mounted between glass and board. During this process the verso was obscured; if there was a text on the verso, a gap would be left in the backing or secondary support and a glass window would be cut into the back board of the frame, leaving the writing visible (although faint texts were sometimes not noticed and were covered over). Unfortunately, these unsupported areas have weakened over the years and some of the backings have deteriorated owing to the poor quality of the paper and board used. These can, in turn, cause damage to the papyri. In many cases the old backings can be removed by controlled use of humidity. As most of the papyri are fragile, the section to be treated is usually faced with a temporary lining before the process of removing it is begun. This facing supports the papyrus during the treatment and is removed as soon as a new support of 'conservation grade' materials has been attached. Sometimes, however, papyri are too delicate for the old backing to be removed.

As previously mentioned, the Ramesseum Papyri were a collection of very fragile and fragmentary rolls found in 1896. At first it was thought that the only method of reading the inside of each roll would be to scrape away the layers one by one, copying the text as each layer was exposed (and then destroyed). In the 1900s, however, they were entrusted to Hugo Ibscher, the papyrus conservator at the Egyptian Museum, Berlin, who experimented with a variety of materials and methods as he moved from one roll to the next. He either secured the sheets of papyrus onto a film of gelatin (sometimes with and sometimes without cellulose nitrate adhesive) or laid them directly onto waxed glass. Gelatin film degrades over time and gradually blackens; the film can sometimes be removed, by a similar method to that described above. When cellulose nitrate adhesive is present this can prove very difficult, especially with such fragile papyri. Recent conservation work on Papyrus Ramesseum 18 revealed that in this case, the fragments were unrolled and mounted onto celluloid film. Much of the papyrus burnt away before it was acquired by the British Museum in 1956: early celluloid film can sometimes spontaneously ignite and this had happened here.

The most important principles of modern conservation are that treatment should preserve an object, while maintaining its historical integrity and should also be reversible, in case it proves unhelpful or inappropriate in the long term. Very few papyri are complete: most classical papyri are small fragments excavated from rubbish heaps, while more Pharaonic rolls have survived intact, having been placed in dry cemeteries. Nevertheless, fewer than a quarter of the papyri in the Department of Egyptian Antiquities at the British Museum can be considered reasonably complete. Even a perfectly preserved manuscript poses the problem of how to unroll a tightly compacted papyrus, undisturbed for millennia. This can be done by introducing enough moisture to make the material more flexible. In the past, intact papyri were treated as follows: they were

B/w 17420/

53 *Two views of part of a papyrus roll containing copies of despatches from the fortresses in Nubia, written in black with headings in red. Before 1956, the papyrus was unrolled onto a film of cellulose nitrate, which has subsequently burnt, as the more recent photograph (below) shows. Late Middle Kingdom, c.1800 BC, from Thebes. H. 12.5 cm. EA 10771.*

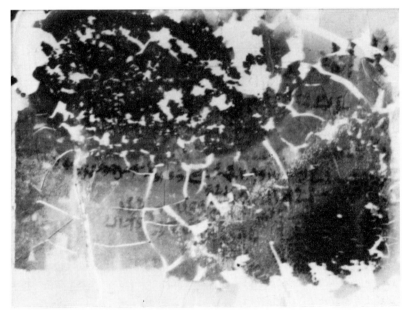

wrapped in damp cloth or blotting paper, left for several hours and then unrolled in stages, flattening each unrolled section between dry blotting paper and glass. The modern method is in principle the same, but moisture can be more subtly introduced by using water vapour; this involves controlled amounts of moisture such as do not affect the ink or any pigments.

Other problems can be posed by carbonized papyrus whose body has been reduced to a mass of black and brittle compressed sheets (rather like a log of wood reduced to charcoal). Many have been unrolled in the past using a wide variety of methods, including the use of a heated lamp. The rolls have sometimes been smeared with very dilute animal glue and then

54

54   *Fragment from a carbonised papyrus roll known as the Tanis Geographical Papyrus; the hieroglyphic text can still be discerned in raking light. Roman Period, second century AD, from Tanis. H. 10.5 cm. EA 10673.2, detail.*

laid down on thin cow gut as a backing. Machinery to help this process included a curious cylinder (involving string, fish glue, and gut) which was devised by the scholar Father Piaggio who in the 1750s worked on some of the carbonized classical papyri from Herculaneum. It is often still possible to read the burnt texts once they are unrolled, either by using a raking light (which shows the reflective surface of the ink) or infrared light. Some of the carbonized rolls that were discovered at Tanis have still not been unrolled.

Some rolls are artificial bundles made up in modern times from various scraps of potentially valuable old papyri. These scraps can usually be separated, or 'unrolled', using water vapour, but if the adhesive used to stick them together is (for example) an animal glue, the process can be more difficult.

Pigments present yet another set of problems, especially when their particles have become loose or are flaking off. The pigments were applied as watercolours; ground earth colours were mixed with a binding substance such as gum arabic. This binding substance can degrade with time and sometimes no longer holds the particles of pigment together. Some pigments were ground fairly roughly, which meant that the particles were rather large and hence more likely to become detached. Modern handling and the process of unrolling have often lead to pigment-loss, although many illustrated papyri retain colours that are still remarkably fresh. The green and blue pigments, however, tend to be copper based and have often blackened; this discoloration can be offset onto other parts of the roll, causing additional stains. In some cases, these pigments have decayed into corrosive compounds which have eaten through the area of papyrus that was once coloured. Loose and flaking pigments can be

37, 38,
V–VIII

55, VI

55 *The verso-end of the papyrus roll containing the* Book of the Dead *of* Amenhotep, *on the verso side. On the left there is a single line of hieroglyphic text containing an offering formula. The stains and holes are caused by the corrosive effects of a copper-based green pigment (compare the recto, colour plate VI). Early Eighteenth Dynasty, c.1450 BC, from Thebes. H. 34 cm. EA 10489.16, detail.*

consolidated in various ways; most involve the introduction of adhesives into and under the layer of pigment. This difficult task often requires the use of a solvent to allow the adhesive to penetrate. Another major problem is the fact that certain pigments are sensitive to light. The yellows and oranges on Egyptian illustrated papyri often contain sulphides of arsenic (orpiment and realgar respectively) which are particularly sensitive and can fade away almost completely.

Various stains can disfigure a papyrus. Funerary papyri are prone to extensive staining from the resin poured over a mummy at burial or from fluids from the body. There is always a dilemma whether to try to reduce the stains, since these can themselves provide valuable information. A vital part of the history of Papyrus Chester Beatty 9 (BM EA 10689) is provided by the dirt on its surface (see p. 64). As with all work on papyri, much consultation is necessary between curators and conservators before any treatment is undertaken.

Disfiguration can also be caused by salts in the soil from which a papyrus was excavated. In a contaminated papyrus, these salts absorb moisture and can crystallise on its surface, causing it to decay or disintegrate. Once the crystals have formed they can be picked out with fine tweezers under a microscope. If they are too embedded for this they can be washed out, either by immersion in water or by laying the papyrus on damp blotting paper, followed by controlled drying. However, some salts are insoluble or only partly soluble; in this case the papyrus should be kept in a stable and relatively low humidity to prevent the absorption of any more moisture and the crystallisation of more salts.

General embrittlement, causing fractures, loss and holes, is the commonest form of damage to papyri, but the situation is rarely hopeless. A roll that has been partially reduced to fragments can often be reconstructed by examining the shapes of the fragments. Patterns of damage can be very informative and the lines of fractures in a letter, for example, often reveal how it was folded for carrying. The damage done by decay or by insect tunnels can be used to calculate how tightly the papyrus had been rolled when last used, and from the spaces between holes it is sometimes possible to estimate how much of an incomplete roll has been lost.

One unexpected source of papyri is the material known as 'cartonnage'. Its potential was realised in 1826 by the collector and first curator of the Berlin Museum Egyptian collections, Giuseppe Passalacqua. In Pharaonic Egypt, mummy masks, coffins and some other objects were made from layers of linen and gesso, a sort of ancient layered papier mâché, which could then be painted. Later, in the Ptolemaic Period, discarded papyri were used instead of linen. Cartonnage is best known as a source of classical texts, although the papyri used included hieratic documents. In the past, acids or enzymes were used to separate the papyrus layers, but this process destroyed the painted gesso layer and created the dilemma of whether to preserve the painted mask or to destroy it in the hope of finding papyri. New techniques are being developed to peel the layers of papyrus away from the inside of a mask, without damaging the painted outer surface, but it is still a difficult task.

Despite all these techniques, the modern reader is often faced with a mass of small fragments, rather like a jigsaw. In some cases the pieces can be reassembled by the contents of text or design, particularly by examining the minute traces on the very edges. These are, however, often insufficient, especially when the fragments come from a copy of a hitherto unknown text. For example, the rearrangement of some Seventeenth Dynasty fragments (BM EA 10475) that contained two otherwise unknown literary texts was problematic, while it was very straightforward to reassemble some very similar fragments (BM EA 74125) with well known spells from the *Book of the Dead*. It would be impossible to repair and rejoin such pieces as BM EA 10475 with any certainty without the help of the fibres that are a characteristic feature of papyrus. These criss-cross fibres form an irregular pattern in a sheet that is as distinctive as a thumb print and this allows 'fibre matching'. In this, two fragments from the same sheet that might join are placed side by side to see whether the fibres

56 Papyrus bearing a contract in demotic for a sale of a room. The evenly spaced holes were caused by damage to the rolled document; they become larger toward the right end, which was on the unprotected outside of the roll. Ptolemaic Period, 136 BC, from Thebes. H. 9.5 cm. EA 10390, detail.

57 A cartonnage image of the goddess Nut placed on the breast of a mummy. It was manufactured from part of a papyrus roll. When the cartonnage was separated in modern times, a fragment of the original text, a demotic account, was recovered. Ptolemaic Period, c.200–100 BC, provenance unknown. H. 11.5 cm. EA 10838.

58 *Example of fragments joined with the help of the fibres; the text is an otherwise unknown literary composition, and therefore of limited help in reassembling the papyrus. Second Intermediate Period, c.1600 BC, provenance unknown. EA 10475, detail.*

match and whether the fragments do join directly. Some reassembly can be done with the naked eye. Viewing the fibres in different lights, including raking light, is helpful and one Oxford papyrologist considered that the light was best when snow was on the ground. Examination is helped by the use of a low-powered microscope and a light table, which provides a diffuse light underneath the fragments, makes the lattice of fibres more clearly visible. When two fragments do not join directly it can still be possible to establish a relationship between them (for example, that they belonged to the same line of text).

However, sometimes a papyrus can have a fibre pattern that is so regular that it is not very distinctive, or it can be too opaque to allow the aid of a light-table. Two fragments from different sheets of a roll will, of course, have unmatchable fibres. Sheet joins pose another problem, as fragments from a join are too thick for any pattern to be easily detected. When a papyrus has been torn or very vigorously palimpsested, the fibres can be distorted, making the process of matching more complicated. Despite these limitations, the technique is invaluable. It was developed for Greek papyri and Egyptology has benefited from these experiences. For example, John Barns, who was accomplished in both disciplines, reassembled the only known copy of *The Discourse of Sasobek* (Papyrus Ramesseum 1, now BM EA 10754) by this method, despite the added difficulty that the fragments were too delicate to be removed from their original mounting.

When the arrangement of the fragments has been decided, the ones that join are attached to each other with small strips of Japanese paper (a good quality paper with long fibres). These paper tabs are a similar colour to the papyrus and so are not distracting; the adhesive used is wheat starch paste. The joined fragments are then tabbed down to a sheet of glass in the same way. The papyrus is then placed between two sheets of glass and sealed with tape. In some collections, perspex has been adopted because it is lighter and less fragile; if a papyrus mounted in glass was

59

26, 29, 37, 58

60

59 *Conservation of a* Book of the Dead; *the fragments can be reassembled from the remains of a roll, with the help both of the text and of the pattern of fibres. Third Intermediate Period, c.950* BC, *from Thebes.* H. *27 cm.* EA *10988.*

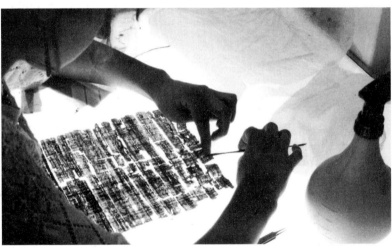

60 *Conservation of a papyrus sheet bearing the text of a letter. The light-table reveals the fibre pattern, ensuring accurate realignment of the fragments. Late Twentieth Dynasty, c.1100* BC, *from Thebes.*

dropped, the glass might smash and its broken edges damage the manuscript. However, perspex is flexible and can warp or bend, leaving the papyrus unsupported inside; more seriously, static electricity can create problems if the frame of perspex needs to be opened again. It is also more prone to scratching. For these reasons glass is still generally preferred.

For storage and display, a temperature of 20° C and a relative humidity of 50–55% are considered satisfactory for organic materials such as papyrus (this prevents dangers including mould); rapid fluctuations of temperature and humidity must be avoided. Light is another important factor, especially the ultraviolet part of the daylight spectrum which contains high energy radiation that can cause reactions in some materials. A special film can be applied to glass frames to help protect the papyrus from some of the harmful rays. When exposed to light, papyrus will bleach: two sheets from the same papyrus, one of which has been displayed for many years and the other kept in the reserve collection, can show a great difference in colour and tone. The problem is worse for

61

B/w 273742 & B/w 272911.

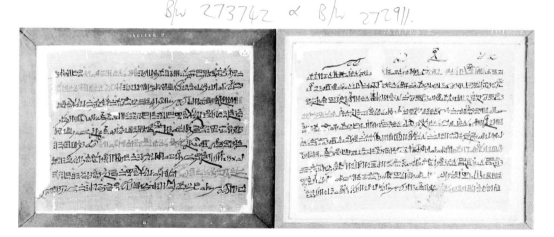

61 *The effects of light on papyrus: these two frames are from the same papyrus roll, but the right one has been displayed in daylight for a prolonged period. The papyrus is bleached, making the text stand out more, but leaving the material weakened. Late Nineteenth Dynasty, c.1225 BC, from Saqqara. H. 21.5 cm. EA 10182.8 and 10182.2.*

painted papyri with light-sensitive pigments. In many respects the ideal conditions for papyri are found in storerooms as dark as the tombs in which many of them were originally deposited. Although it is vital to make papyri accessible to the public, for these reasons only a selection can be put on display, and only in controlled conditions, with low light and constant temperature levels.

REVIVALS

Revivals in papyrus manufacture over the past two centuries have been sporadic. In the late eighteenth century the explorer James Bruce experimented with Sudanese papyrus. Also in the eighteenth century the Sicilian Saverio Landolina produced an acceptable writing material from Syracusan papyrus; he sent letters on his papyrus to scholars such as the courtier Heyne at Göttingen where one, dated 23 December 1785, can still be seen in the library. Papyrus production continued in Sicily, but on a small scale. A Syracusan society of papyrus manufacturers was founded in 1922 but survived only four years, leaving exceptional individuals, such as some sisters from the Naro family, to continue the tradition.

62

Late nineteenth-century research attracted the interest of the Khedive of Egypt, but his plans to manufacture papyrus foundered because the plant absorbs considerable amounts of fresh water, which was a limited commodity in the densely populated Delta. In the twentieth century the production of papyrus took on greater impetus, both in Sicily and in Egypt. Two institutions are notable: the Papyrus Institute and museums of H. Ragab in Egypt and the papyrus museum of Corrado Basile at Syracuse, which promote research and supply papyri for the tourist market. These initiatives have aided practical experiments and research into techniques of manufacture.

COLOPHON

Although so fragile, papyrus preserved a significant portion of the records of humanity, including Europe's classical heritage which was originally transmitted on papyri. Papyrus alone preserves many aspects of ancient Egyptian culture that were excluded from monumental records on stone, revealing both practical realities and a less idealised, but more poetic, vision of the world. Despite the fact that papyri have often been reduced to small fragments which are easy to overlook, it is difficult to resist the excitement that Vivant Denon experienced during Napoleon's expedition in 1798–9, when he uncovered an example of these frail rivals of the pyramids. He speculated:

The oldest of all the books in the known world ... What could be its contents? Was it the history of this personage, the remarkable events of his life? ... or did this precious roll contain maxims, prayers, or the history of some discovery?

62 *A sheet of modern papyrus with a hand-coloured print depicting the flowering papyrus plant as found in the marshes near Syracuse. Nineteenth century* AD, *from Sicily.* H. *25.8 cm.* EA *36832.*

Chronological Table

PREDYNASTIC PERIODS

c.4500–3000 BC

EARLY DYNASTIC

Dynasties 1–3

c.3100–2613 BC

OLD KINGDOM

Dynasties 4–8

c.2613–2160 BC

FIRST INTERMEDIATE PERIOD

Dynasties 9–10 and Dynasty 11
in southern Upper Egypt

c.2160–2025 BC

MIDDLE KINGDOM

Dynasties 11–13 over all Egypt

c.2025–1700 BC

SECOND INTERMEDIATE PERIOD

Dynasty 13 over Upper Egypt
and Dynasties 14–17

c.1700–1550 BC

NEW KINGDOM

Dynasty 18

c.1550–1295 BC

Dynasty 19

c.1295–1186 BC

Dynasty 20

c.1186–1069 BC

THIRD INTERMEDIATE PERIOD

Dynasties 21–23

c.1069–727 BC

LATE PERIOD

Dynasties 24–30 and Persian occupation

c.727–332 BC

PTOLEMAIC PERIOD

332–30 BC

ROMAN PERIOD

30 BC–AD 330

BYZANTINE PERIOD

AD 330–641

ISLAMIC PERIOD

After AD 641

The Coptic Period covers the fourth to eighth centuries AD when early Christian art has its own distinctive form in Egypt: Coptic manuscripts continued to be produced after the disappearance of Coptic art.

Citations

References are given for the texts that are quoted in each chapter. For the principal literary texts translations can be found in the works by Lichtheim and Simpson, Faulkner and Wente, and for the funerary literature (*Book of the Dead, Coffin Texts* and *Pyramid Texts*) in the works by Faulkner, cited in the Bibliography.

Chapter 1
Pliny the Elder, *Natural History*, xiii, 68

Tale of Sinuhe line B 122: R. Koch, *Die Erzäahlung des Sinuhe*, 48. Brussels, Fondation Egyptologique Reine Elisabeth 1990.

Hymn to the Inundation, sections 8g–h: W. Helck, *Der Text des 'Nilhymnus'*, 48–51. Kleine Ägyptische Texte; Wiesbaden, Otto Harrassowitz 1972.

Beating papyrus: Papyrus Anastasi 3 (BM EA 10246), col. 5, lines 8–9: text in A. H. Gardiner, *Late-Egyptian Miscellanies*, 26. Bibliotheca Aegyptiaca 7; Brussels, Fondation Egyptologique Reine Elisabeth 1937. Translation in R. A. Caminos, *Late-Egyptian Miscellanies*, 92–3. London, Geoffrey Cumberlege for Oxford University Press 1954.

Annals of Thutmes III from the temple at Karnak: hieroglyphic text in K. Sethe, *Urkunden des Ägyptischen Altertums*, IV. Abteilung. *Urkunden der 18. Dynastie*, 662, lines 5–6. Leipzig, J. C. Hinrichs 1907.

Chapter 2
Clement of Alexandria: *Stromata*, V, 4, 20

Papyrus Anastasi 1 col. 1, line 6: H.-W. Fischer-Elfert, *Die Satirische Streitschrift des Papyrus Anastasi* 1, 24. Kleine Ägyptische Texte (2nd edn); Wiesbaden, Otto Harrassowitz 1992.

Words of Neferti, sections 2o–q: W. Helck, *Die Prophezeiung des Nfr.tj*, 12–15. Kleine Ägyptische Texte; Wiesbaden, Otto Harrassowitz 1970.

Ostracon Petrie 62; translation after E. Wente, *Letters from Ancient Egypt*, 165. Atlanta, Scholars Press 1990.

Pyramid Text: PT 476, in the tombs of Pepy I and II and Meryra: K. Sethe, *Die Altaegyptischen Pyramidentexte* II, 32, sections 954a–b. Leipzig, J. C. Hinrichs 1910.

Coffin Text: from *Coffin Text* spell 540 'Spell for becoming a Scribe of Hathor' attested on a coffin fragment from Meir; text in A. de Buck and A. H. Gardiner, *The Egyptian Coffin Texts* VI, 135 sections q–r. Chicago, University of Chicago Press 1956.

Palimpsest: P. Holmiensis γ, lines 160–1; cited by C. H. Roberts and T. C. Skeat, *The Birth of the Codex*, 17. London, Oxford University Press for the British Academy 1987.

Chapter 3

Eloquent Peasant line B1 336: R. B. Parkinson, *The Tale of the Eloquent Peasant*, 43. Oxford, Griffith Institute 1991.

Papyrus Chester Beatty 4 (BM EA 10684), verso col.3, line 1: A. H. Gardiner, *Hieratic Papyri in the British Museum: 3rd series II. Chester Beatty Gift*, 39, pl.19. London, British Museum 1935.

Papyrus Lansing (BM EA 9994) col. 2, lines 1–3: text in A. H. Gardiner, *Late-Egyptian Miscellanies*, 100. Bibliotheca Aegyptiaca 7; Brussels, Fondation Egyptologique Reine Elisabeth 1937. Translation in R. A. Caminos, *Late-Egyptian Miscellanies*, 374. London, Geoffrey Cumberlege for Oxford University Press 1954.

Papyrus of Nespasef, in Metropolitan Museum of Art, New York, unpublished.

Love song: Papyrus Chester Beatty 1, col. 16, line 9: in M. V. Fox, *The Song of Songs and the Ancient Egyptian Love Songs*, 400–401. Wisconsin, University of Wisconsin Press 1985. First edition of the text by A. H. Gardiner, *The Library of A. Chester Beatty. Description of a Hieratic Papyrus with a Mythological Story, Love-Songs, and Other Miscellaneous Texts. The Chester Beatty Papyri, No. 1*. London, Emery Walker 1931.

Neferhotep stela lines 6–7: in W. Helck, *Historisch-Biographische Texte der 2. Zwischenzeit und neue texte der 18. Dynastie*, 22. Kleine Ägyptische Texte; Wiesbanden, Otto Harrassowitz 1983. No translation in the accessible anthologies.

Late Ramesside Letter with comment on Pharaoh: Berlin 10487, recto line 9-verso line 1: Jaroslav Černý, *Late Ramesside Letters*, 36. Bibliotheca Aegyptiaca 9; Brussels, Fondation Egyptologique Reine Elisabeth 1939. Translation in E. Wente, *Letters from Ancient Egypt*, 183. Atlanta, Scholars Press 1990.

Late Ramesside Letter concerning rain damage to papyri: BM EA 10326, lines 20–2: Jaroslav Černý, *Late Ramesside Letters*, 18–19. Bibliotheca Aegyptiaca 9; Brussels, Fondation Egyptologique Reine Elisabeth 1939. Translation in E. Wente, *Letters from Ancient Egypt*, 191. Atlanta, Scholars Press 1990.

V. Denon, *Travels in Upper and Lower Egypt* (trans. A.Aikin) II, 217–18. London, Longman and Rees 1803.

Chapter 4

Shabaka Stone (BM EA 498), K. Sethe, *Dramatische Texte zu altäagyptischen Mysterienspielen I: Das 'Denkmal Memphistischer Theologie' der Schabakostein des Britischen Museums*. Leipzig, J. C. Hinrichs, 1928. Translation in Miriam Lichtheim, *Ancient Egyptian Literature I, The Old and Middle Kingdoms*, Berkeley, University of California Press 1973, 51–7.

Bibliography

S. ALEXANDER, 'Notes on the Use of Gold-leaf in Egyptian Papyri'. *Journal of Egyptian Archaeology* 51 (1965), 48–52 (with an addendum by T. G. H. James).

A. S. ATIYA (ed.), *The Coptic Encyclopedia* (8 vols). New York, Macmillan 1991.

J. BAINES, 'Literacy and Ancient Egyptian Society'. *Man* (n.s) 18 (1983), 572–99.

J. W. B. BARNS, *Five Ramesseum Papyri*. Oxford University Press 1956.

C. BASILE, 'Metodo usato dagli antichi egizi per la fabbricazione e la preservazione della carta-papiro'. *Aegyptus* 57 (1977), 190–9.

M. L. BIERBRIER (ed.), *Papyrus: Structure and Usage* (British Museum Occasional Paper 60). London, British Museum Publications 1986.

L. BORCHARDT, 'Das Dienstgebäude des Auswartigen Amtes unter den Ramessiden'. *Zeitschrift für Ägyptische Sprache und Altertumskunde* 44 (1907), 59–61.

G. BURKARD, 'Bibliotheken im alten Ägypten' in *Bibliothek: Forschung und Praxis* 4 (1980), 79–115.

A. BÜLOW-JAKOBSEN, 'Papyrus in Three layers? P. Haun. 1 (inv. no. 5n)'. *Chronique d'Egypte* 53 (no. 105, 1978), 158–61.

R. A. CAMINOS, 'Some comments on the reuse of papyrus', in M. L. Bierbrier, op.cit., 43–61.

THE EARL OF CARNARVON and H. CARTER, *Five years' Exploration at Thebes. A record of work done 1907–1911*. London and New York, Henry Frowde for Oxford University Press 1912.

H. CARTER and A. H. GARDINER, 'The Tomb of Ramesses IV and the Turin Plan of a Royal Tomb'. *Journal of Egyptian Archaeology* 4 (1917), 130–58.

J. ČERNÝ, *Paper and Books in Ancient Egypt*. London, H. K. Lewis for University College London 1952.

W. V. DAVIES, *Egyptian Hieroglyphs*. London, British Museum Publications 1987.

A. DONNITHORNE, 'The conservation of papyrus in the British Museum'. In M. L. Bierbrier, op.cit..

R. O. FAULKNER, *The Ancient Egyptian Book of the Dead* (revised edn C. A. R. Andrews). London, British Museum Publications 1985.
The Ancient Egyptian Coffin Texts (3 vols). Warminster, Aris and Phillips 1973–8.
The Ancient Egyptian Pyramid Texts. Oxford, Clarendon Press 1969.

A. H. GARDINER, *Hieratic Papyri in the British Museum: 3rd series* II. *Chester Beatty Gift*. London, British Museum 1935.
The Ramesseum Papyri. Oxford University Press for Griffith Institute 1955.

J. A. HARELL and V. MAX BROWN, 'The Oldest Surviving Topographical Map from Ancient Egypt: (Turin Papyri 1879, 1899, and 1969)'. *Journal of the American Research Center in Egypt* 29 (1992), 81–105.

T. HARRISON, *The Trackers of Oxyrhynchus: The Delphi Text 1988*. London, Faber and Faber 1990.

I. H. M. HENDRICKS, 'Pliny, Historia Naturalis XIII, 74–82 and the manufacture of papyrus'. *Zeitschrift für Papyrologie und Epigraphik* 38 (1980), 121–36.

'More about the manufacture of papyrus'. *Atti del XVII Congresso internazionale di Papirologia I*, 31–7. Naples 1984.

T. G. H. JAMES, *Egyptian Painting and Drawing in the British Museum*. London, British Museum Publications 1983.

JAC J. JANSSEN, *Commodity Prices from the Ramessid Period: An Economic Study of the Village of Necropolis Workmen at Thebes*. Leiden, E. J. Brill 1975.

G. JEQUIER, *Les Frises d'Objets des Sarcophages du Moyen Empire* (Memoires publiés par les membres de l'Institut Français d'Archéologie Orientale au Caire 47). Cairo, Imprimérie de l'Institut Français d'Archéologie Orientale 1921.

N. LEWIS, *Papyrus in Classical Antiquity*. Oxford, Clarendon Press 1974
'The Demise of the Demotic Document: When and Why'. *Journal of Egyptian Archaeology* 79 (1993), 276–81.

M. LICHTHEIM, *Ancient Egyptian Literature: A Book of Readings* (3 vols). University of California Press, Berkeley, 1973–80.

A. LUCAS, *Ancient Egyptian Materials and Industries* (4th edn, revised, J. R. Harris). London, Edward Arnold 1962.

E. MENEI, 'Remarques sur la fabrication des rouleaux de papyrus: précisions sur la formation et l'assemblage des feuillets'. *Revue d'Égyptologie* 44 (1993), 185–8.

W. L. MORAN, *The Amarna Letters*. Baltimore and London, John Hopkins University Press 1992.

R. B. PARKINSON, *Voices from Ancient Egypt: An Anthology of Middle Kingdom Writings*. London, British Museum Press 1991.

T. S. PATTIE and E. G. TURNER, *The Written Word on Papyrus*. London, British Museum Publications for British Library Board 1974.

P. W. PESTMAN, 'Who were the owners, in the "Community of Workmen", of the Chester Beatty Papyri?' in R. J. Demarée & J. J. Janssen (eds), *Gleanings from Deir el-Medina*, 155–72. Leiden, Nederlands Instituut voor het Nabije Oosten 1982.

G. POSENER, 'Sur l'emploi de l'encre rouge dans les manuscrits égyptiens'. *Journal of Egyptian Archaeology* 37 (1951), 75–80.

P. POSENER-KRIEGER, 'Les tablettes en terre crue de Balat'. *Bibliologia: Elementa ad librorum studia pertinentia* 12, 41–52.

H. RAGAB, 'The quality of recently manufactured papyrus as compared with ancient Egyptian papyrus'. *Proceedings of the 18th International Congress of Papyrology* II, 513–23. Athens, 1988.

M. J. RAVEN, *Papyrus: van bies tot boekrol*. Zutphen, Terra 1984.

L. D. REYNOLDS and N. G. WILSON, *Scribes and Scholars*. Oxford, Clarendon Press 1974 (1st edn 1968).

C. H. ROBERTS and T. C. SKEAT, *The Birth of the Codex*. London, Oxford University Press for the British Academy 1987.

G. ROBINS and C. SHUTE, *The Rhind Mathematical Papyrus: an Ancient Egyptian Text*. London, British Museum Publications 1987.

S. SAUNERON, *Textes et langages de l'Egypte pharaonique: cent cinquante années de recherches 1822–1972. Hommage à Jean-François Champollion* (3 vols) (Bibliothèque d'Etude 64). Cairo, Institut Français d'Archéologie Orientale du Caire 1974.

A. SCHLOTT, *Schrift und Schreiber im Alten Ägypten*. Munich, Beck 1989.

W. K. SIMPSON, R. O. FAULKNER and E. WENTE, *The Literature of Ancient Egypt: An Anthology of Stories, Instructions, and Poetry* (2nd edn). New Haven and London, Yale University Press 1973.

H. S. SMITH and H. M. STEWART, 'The Gurob Shrine Papyrus'. *Journal of Egyptian Archaeology* 70 (1984), 54–64.

P. VAN SUMMERS, *Where Writing Starts: The Analysis of Action Applied to the Historical Development of Writing*. Fourth International Graphonomics Society Conference, Trondheim 1989.

V. TACKHOLM and M. DRAR, *Flora of Egypt Vol. II Angiospermae, part Monocotyledones: Cyperaceae – Juncaceae* (Bulletin of the Faculty of Sciences 28). Cairo, Fouad I University Press 1950.

W. J. TAIT, 'Guidelines and borders in Demotic papyri', in M. L. Bierbrier, op.cit., 63–89.
'Rush and reed: the Pens of Egyptian and Greek Scribes', in *Proceedings of the 17th International Congress of Papyrology* II, 477–81. Athens, 1988.

E. TURNER, *Greek Papyri: An Introduction*. Oxford, Clarendon Press 1980 (1st edn 1968).

P. VERNUS, 'Schreibtafel' in W. Helck (ed.), *Lexikon der Ägyptologie* V, 703–9. Wiesbaden, Otto Harrassowitz 1984.

J. VERGOTE, 'L'étymologie du mot "papyrus"'. *Chronique d'Egypte* 60 (1985), 393–7.

S. P. VLEEMING, 'La phase initiale du démotique ancien'. *Chronique d'Egypte* 56 (1981), 31–48.

A. WALLERT, 'The reconstruction of papyrus manufacture: a preliminary investigation'. *Studies in Conservation* 34 (1989), 1–8.

E. F. WENTE, *Letters from Ancient Egypt*. Atlanta, Scholars Press 1990.

H. E. WINLOCK, 'A Set of Egyptian Writing Materials'. *Bulletin of the Metropolitan Museum of Art New York* 9 (1914), 181–2.

Papyri Today

Sheets of modern papyri are manufactured by, among others, Dr H. Ragab's Institute in Cairo. These are brightly painted with modern versions of Egyptian designs for the tourist market and are widely available in Egypt; they are also exported to Britain. For anyone wishing to write their own papyrus, sheets can be obtained from artists' suppliers specialising in fine papers. These are often more speckled than pure papyrus, having been made from banana leaves. With such a sheet, an italic pen and a box of water colours, passable imitations can be produced.

Papyri in the Department of Egyptian Antiquities, British Museum

The following list includes, with the papyri in the Department of Egyptian Antiquities, all linen and leather manuscripts within the main sequence of numbers BM EA 9900 to 10999 (within that sequence some numbers, e.g. BM EA 10540, 10675 and 10677, are vacant). A suffix number (e.g. .2) indicates the modern sheet number of the papyrus.

Since 1840 Greek papyri and the bulk of the Coptic manuscripts have been assigned to the former Department of Manuscripts, now part of the British Library.

HIEROGLYPHIC AND HIERATIC MANUSCRIPTS

(on papyrus unless otherwise stated)

ROYAL TEXTS
Great Harris Papyrus: 9999 (this posthumous statement of good deeds of King Ramses III includes administrative lists as well as religious and literary passages).

TEXTS OF DAILY LIFE

Administrative
Old Kingdom: 10735.
Middle Kingdom: 10371+10435 verso, 10752 recto, 10756 verso, 10771, 10916.
18th Dynasty:10056.
Ramesside: 9997 recto, 10061, 10189, 10204, 10309 verso, 10333–4, 10341, 10400–1, 10447, 10551, 10696 verso, 10776–8, 73668.
Third Intermediate Period: 10106, 10798.

Legal
Ramesside: 10055, 10335, 10568, 10950.
Ramesside Tomb Robbery papyri: 10052–4, 10068, 10221, (fragments 10325 and 10342 now rejoined to previous numbers), 10383, 10403.
Abnormal hieratic: 10113, 10432, 10800.

Letters
Old Kingdom/First Intermediate Period: 10901 (Letter to the Dead).
Middle Kingdom: 10549, 10567, 10864.
18th Dynasty: 10102–4, 10107.
Ramesside: 10069, 10248, 10779, 73666.
Late Ramesside: 10100–1, 10190, 10273, 10284, 10287, 10300, 10302, 10326, 10373, 10375, 10411–2, (10440 part of 10302), 10416–9, 10429–30, 10433, 71511.
Third Intermediate Period: 71507, 71509.

LITERATURE

Dream Books
Ramesside manuscript (copy of Middle Kingdom text ?): 10683 recto.

Mathematical
Second Intermediate Period: 10057–8, 10250 (leather).

Onomastica and related texts

Third Intermediate Period: 10202, 10379 (leather), 10795.

Roman Period: 10672–3 ('Tanis Sign Papyrus' and 'Geographical Papyrus').

Texts for Health ('magical/medical texts')

Middle Kingdom: 10752 verso, 10756 recto, 10757–8, 10760–70.

Second Intermediate Period: 10902.

New Kingdom: 9997 verso, 10042, 10059, 10085+10105, 10309 recto, 10685 verso, 10686–8, 10689 verso, 10690–3, 10695, 10696 recto, 10698 verso, 10731–2.

Third Intermediate Period (oracular amulets): 10083, 10251, 10308, 10313, 10320–1, 10587, 10730, 10899.

Late Period: 9961, 10547.

Greek script, Middle Egyptian (?): 10808.

Illustrated papyri (for funerary examples, see under funerary texts)

New Kingdom: 9930–1 (funerary?) 10016 ('Satirical'); 74100 (battle scene); 74102 (leather).

Late Period: 10866.

Literary

Middle Kingdom: 10274, 10371+10435 recto, 10754–5.

Second Intermediate Period: 10475.

New Kingdom: 9994, 10060, 10181–5, 10222, 10243–7, 10249, 10258 (leather), 10509, 10566, 10682, 10683 verso, 10684, 10685, 10697, 10698 recto, 10699, 10780, 73667.

Third Intermediate Period: 10298 ('Schoolbook'), 10474, 10797(?).

Late Period: 69574.

RELIGIOUS TEXTS

Rituals

Middle Kingdom: 10610 (kingship), 10753 (burial), 10759 (Sobek hymns).

New Kingdom: 10689 (temple), 10819 (funerary cult).

Late Period (excluding those taken or copied for funerary equipment): 10651–3.

Roman Period (hieroglyphic texts of uncertain content): 10879, 10893.

Funerary

BD indicates Book of the Dead: numbers of chapters refer to the editions by E. Naville, Das Ägyptische Todtenbuch der XVIII. bis XX.

Dynastie (Berlin, A. Asher 1886) and W. Pleyte, Chapitres supplémentaires du Livre des Morts (Leiden, E. J. Brill 1881).

Middle Kingdom: 10676 (Coffin Texts).

Second Intermediate Period: (10553 facsimile of texts on a coffin), 10706 (linen).

New Kingdom, BD: 9900–1, 9905, 9913–4, 9926–9, 9933–7, 9939–40, 9943, 9945, 9949–50, 9953–9, 9962, 9964–5, 9968, 9971–2, 9988, 9990–1, 10009, 10021 (leather), 10217, 10281 (leather), 10466–7, 10470–2, 10473 (leather, start of 10471), 10477, 10489, 10704, 10708 (linen), 10736–8, 70896, 73669, 74126, 74131, 74134.

New Kingdom, BD chapter 168 (Naville): 9966, 10478.

Third Intermediate Period, BD: 9903–4, 9918–19, 9932, 9938, 9941, 9948, 9969, 9974, 9992, 10010, 10013–14, 10020, 10029, 10031, 10035–6, 10040–1, 10044, 10062–4, 10084, 10093–4, 10096, 10119, 10195 (?), 10203, 10207, 10307, 10312, (fragments 10324 part of 10064), 10327–30, 10339, 10448, 10541, 10554, 10617, 10743, 10747, 10793, 10988, 73665, 73981–2, 74129–30, 74135–6.

Third Intermediate Period, BD chapter 166 (Pleyte): 10422–3, 10562, 74130.

Third Intermediate Period, Litany of Ra: 10006, 10011.

Third Intermediate Period, Amduat: 9970, 9975, 9979–85, 9987, 10000–1, 10012, 10019, 10024, 10267, 10278–9, 10330 (second part), 10674, 10742, 10745–6.

Third Intermediate Period, vignette papyri: 10002–5, 10007–8, 10018.

Third Intermediate Period, BD texts with Book of Caverns vignettes: 10490.

Late Period, BD: 9902, 9906–12, 9920–1, 9923–5, 9944, 9946–7, 9951–2, 9960, 9963, 9967, 9973, 9976, 9986, (10015 photographs of a papyrus in Athens), 10017, 10030, 10032–4, 10037–9, 10043, 10045, 10066–7, 10082A-B, 10086–9, 10092, 10095, 10097–9, 10193, 10197, 10200, 10205, 10210–1, 10213–15, 10218–20, 10253, 10257, 10268, 10272, 10280, 10289, 10293–5, 10301–1a, 10305–6, 10310–1, 10315–16, 10318, 10322–3, 10332, 10336, 10368 (10369 is facsimile of 10368), 10370, 10465, 10469, 10479, 10485, 10539, 10545–6, 10548, 10558, 10700, 10702–3, 10719, 10733–4, 10739–40, 10751, 10784,

10796, 10805, 10844, 10891, 10896, 69012, 73670–3, 74127–9, 74132–3.

Late Period, *BD* on linen: 9917, 9922, 9942, 10028, 10046–7, 10065, 10126, 10143–80, 10186–7, 10212, 10265–6, 10271, 10345–67, 10451–2, 10709, 10711–17, 10781, 10783, 10809, 10826.

Late Period, vignette on papyrus: 10296.

Late Period, vignette on linen: 9989, 10269–70, 10707.

Late Period, religious texts other than *BD* (principally copies of temple rituals): 10022–3, 10048–51, 10081, 10090 (part of 10051), 10188, 10196 (?), 10208–9, 10216, 10252, 10255, 10261, 10288, 10299 (or Third Intermediate Period?), 10317, 10319, 10468, 10544, 10563, 10565, 10569, 10669, 10915, 10919 (?), 10924 (?), 10945–6, 10951, 10963, 10971, 10973, 10977, 71512, 71514, 73983–4.

Roman, *BD*: 10671, 10983.

Roman, religious texts other than *BD* (principally *Documents of Breathing*): 9977–8, 9995, 10091, 10108–12, 10114–16, 10121, 10123–5, 10191–2, 10194, 10198–9, 10201, 10206, 10254, 10256, 10259, 10262–4A, 10275–7, 10282–3, 10285–6, 10290–2, 10303–4, 10314, 10331, 10337 verso, 10338, 10340, 10343–4, 10415, 10718, 71513.

Unopened roll coated in black (resinous?) material (Late Period *BD*?): 10748

MANUSCRIPTS IN OTHER SCRIPTS

Demotic Papyri

Note: these, the published demotic papyri, are principally legal texts, in addition to the well-known literary and mathematical manuscripts. A more detailed breakdown is given in W. Helck (ed.), *Lexikon der Ägyptologie* IV (Wiesbaden, Otto Harrassowitz 1983), 838–50.

Administrative: 10856

Legal: 10026–7, 10071, 10073–5, 10077–9, 10117, 10120, 10223, 10226–7, 10229–30, 10233, 10238, 10240, 10242, 10372, 10377, 10380, 10384, 10386–90, 10392, 10394–5 (10396 facsimile), 10398, 10402, 10404, 10407, (10408 part of 10386; 10409 part of 10372), 10410, 10413, 10425–6, 10437, 10441, (10442 part of 10404), 10446, 10450, 10463–4, 10491, 10500, 10512, 10522–30, 10532, 10535–7, 10561, 10575, 10589, 10591–601, 10607, 10609, 10611–16, 10622, 10624, 10646–50,

10678–9, 10721–8, 10750, 10782, 10789, 10792, 10827–32, 10839, 10845–6, 10851, 10853

Letters: 10231–2, 10405–6.

Mathematical: 10399, 10520, 10794.

Onomasticon: 10852.

Texts for health: 10070 (+ Greek), 10588 (+ Greek).

Literary: 10508, 10822 (Greek on reverse), 10848, 10850.

Funerary : 10072, 10507.

Coptic Manuscripts (on papyrus unless otherwise stated)

Administrative: 10127–42, 10453–62.

Legal: 71021–2.

Letters: 9996, 10577, 10579–80 (?), 10581 (paper), 10582–6, 69496, 74107–8.

Texts for health ('magical'), on leather: 10122, 10376, 10391, 10414, 10434.

Literary (mainly ecclesiastical): 10576, 10578, 10820 (leather), 71005.

Christian codex cover (European?): 10821.

Non-Egyptian texts

Greek administrative: 10531.

Greek, reverse with demotic literary: 10822.

Greek, with demotic texts for health ('magical'): 10070, 10588.

Greek, reverse with Roman Period funerary text: 10292, 10337.

Meroitic: 10816.

All Old Nubian (Christian) texts in the collection are paper or leather manuscripts (71295–305 and 71381).

The Arabic manuscripts 10481–2 were transferred to the Department of Oriental Printed Books and Manuscripts, now part of the British Library.

OTHER MANUSCRIPTS

Samples of Nineteenth-century Papyrus
36829, 36832–3.

Fragments not assigned to one of the above categories

Middle Kingdom: 10772 (fragments from the 'Ramesseum library').

New Kingdom: 10701 (leather), 10694 and 10749 (Ramesside literary or texts for health), 10775, 10778, 74101 (leather).

Fragment with seal (demotic?): 10538.

Small roll: 10590.

Coptic: 10552, 10979, 10982, 10986.

Assorted fragments in one frame: 10705, 10720, 10930, 10933, 10957, 10961, 10972, 10978, 10984–5.

Unregistered in 1994 pending study and framing

Some of these fragments belong with items or groups already numbered, and are therefore not to receive separate new numbers.

Small fragments: New Kingdom literary and *BD*, Third Intermediate Period *BD*, demotic, Roman Period funerary (not *BD*), Coptic. Fragments pasted together in the nineteenth century to fabricate rolls, not yet separated. Carbonized rolls, extremely fragile, not yet separated and placed under glass. Demotic fragments from cartonnage. Coptic, leaves of codices.

Index

Roman numerals in **bold** refer to colour illustrations, Arabic numbers in **bold** to pages with black-and-white illustrations. For specific manuscripts and objects see separate Index of Objects (IO) listed by location and number.